YOUR CHILD IN FILM AND TELEVISION

Allison Cohee

Self-Counsel Press
(a division of)
International Self-Counsel Press
USA   Canada

Self-Counsel Press acknowledges the financial support of the Government of Canada through the Book Publishing Industry Development Program (BPIDP) for our publishing activities.

Printed in Canada.

First edition: 2003

Canadian Cataloguing in Publication Data

Cohee, Allison, 1957-
    Your child in film and television/Allison Cohee.

(Self-counsel reference series)
1-55180-426-3

    1. Child actors. 2. Television acting—vocational guidance. 3. Motion picture acting—Vocational guidance. I. Title. II. Series.
PN1992.8.A3C63 2003   791.45'028'023   C2003-910022-7

791.4307
COH
2003

—M— 5/03 9/3 —

Self-Counsel Press
(a division of)
International Self-Counsel Press Ltd.

1704 N. State Street	1481 Charlotte Road
Bellingham, WA 98225	North Vancouver, BC V7J 1H1
USA	Canada

CONTENTS

INTRODUCTION

Thousands of children find work each year in the film and television industry. Some even find fame and fortune. But behind the glitz of the entertainment industry lies a lot of hard work and a minefield of terms and protocols that you need to learn.

Which is where this guide comes in. My children and I have been involved in the television and film industry for 14 years. I have experienced the boredom of working background, as well as the thrill of seeing my child act with Academy Award winners. My children are not famous, and may never be, but we have had experiences we will cherish for a lifetime.

I developed the questions I was often asked into a course that I taught, and from this course I developed this guide. One of the most disturbing things I hear about is parents spending a lot of money where they need not be spending it. It is heart wrenching to see people getting rich on others' dreams. It is even more distressing to see parents allow the chance of stardom to influence them to do things that could have a detrimental effect on their children. It is even worse to see them allow their children to do these things.

Remember, there is no secret formula that can determine if your child will succeed in film or television. While this guide will

The expression "break a leg" comes from the Shakespearean theater days when an actor was required to bow in the manner of the day by extending the right leg forward and bending the left leg. It was said that if your performance was done well, the audience would applaud for a long time, and you would have to bow deeper. Thus the term "break a leg" means that you should perform so well that you would have to bow so deep that the left leg would have to bend so much it would break!

For other film and television terms, consult the Glossary at the back of this book.

help you navigate that often confusing world, it in no way guarantees or assures your child's success.

As much as it is a fun and exciting industry, film and television will put your skills as a parent to the test. As with any venture you take with your child, your responsibilities as a parent are of the utmost importance. You are responsible for the physical, mental, and emotional well-being of your child. The horror stories and urban myths about children in film are directly related to the parents of the child. If you know the rules, keep in tune with your child, and take care of his or her interests, the road to fame will be an adventure that you can both enjoy — regardless of whether your child becomes the next Haley Joel Osment or simply gets a chance to share in the spotlight.

1

DO YOU HAVE THE TIME TO INVOLVE YOUR CHILD IN FILM OR TELEVISION?

When you decide to involve your child in film and television, you are entering into a world filled with happiness, disappointments, and opportunity. The process of finding an agent, auditioning, and doing the shoot can consume huge amounts of time. Most often, you are making the time commitment without really knowing what the result will be.

But don't be discouraged. Whether your child gets a star on the Walk of Fame or plays a cute "bottom" on a diaper commercial, your commitment to his or her involvement in film and television can pay off for both of you in more than just financial ways. Being involved in the industry can —

☆ boost your and your child's confidence;

☆ help your child grow emotionally and psychologically by tackling new characters and roles;

☆ stimulate your child's imagination through role-playing and acting;

☆ teach your child to deal with disappointment and rejection and to handle success gracefully;

Treat people in the industry with respect and dignity and you will find your child being treated the same way.

☆ develop organizational and time-keeping skills (necessary if you are to schedule auditions, shoots, etc.);

☆ introduce both of you to people from all walks of life and encourage your child to respect others; and

☆ teach your child how to manage money.

Furthermore, working inside the industry takes the illusion out of movies and television. When your child is influenced by what a toy does on a commercial, you can remind him or her of the behind-the-scenes tricks it took to make it look as if the toy is fantastic.

As if you don't have enough outside influences on your parenting skills, the movie business will test them even further. You will have to deal with successes as well as failures and rejections. It can be very hard not to take it personally if your child doesn't get a part — and often more so if he or she does!

Friends and family will have questions and comments about what you are doing — both good or bad. You may even be accused of exploiting your child. Be prepared for all kinds of rhetoric from inside and outside the industry's community. (You will have to deal with "stage moms" that will brag about their children and you will see parents do and say things to their children that will sicken you.)

The film and television industry is a unique environment. Along with the financial rewards of being paid as adults, children are also often treated as such and are expected to meet adult responsibilities. It is not like signing your child up for sports at your local recreation center. There is no nice, "all the children will get a chance to play" attitude.

Being involved in film and television can be a rewarding and interesting way to spend time with your child. Use Checklist 1 to help you determine whether you, your child, and the rest of your family are ready to get involved.

CHECKLIST 1
ARE YOU READY FOR THE FILM AND TELEVISION INDUSTRY?

Questions for parents about *themselves:*

❏ Do you have the support of your spouse?

❏ Do you have the time to devote to taking your child to agents, auditions, and shoots?

❏ Do you have suitable transportation to get to auditions and shoots (which can often run late by hours)?

❏ Are you prepared to travel to remote locations for shoots or into the city for auditions?

❏ Are you tenacious? Are you prepared to keep going to auditions with little encouragement from casting directors?

❏ Do you have the patience to spend a lot of time "hanging around" while your child is auditioning or shooting? Remember, your child should always be in your sight while on and off a film set, and you may have to spend long hours finding ways to keep yourself busy.

❏ Can you keep your feet on the ground and not get caught up in the whole atmosphere of the industry?

Questions for parents about their *child:*

❏ Does your child have an interest in acting or in being involved in a film or commercial?

❏ Will he or she enjoy the experience of auditioning or performing without necessarily needing to become a star?

❏ Does your child have sufficient ability or a particular skill?

❏ Does your child have the patience required to attend numerous auditions and to wait around a set. He or she may have to spend many hours sitting around waiting. Can he or she stay occupied independently?

❏ Will your child handle missing regular school occasionally and having to use a tutor?

❏ Is your child able to take direction?

❏ Does your child have the self-confidence to handle rejection as well as success?

❏ If you have an infant, will he or she be willing to go to a stranger, or does he or she "make shy"?

Questions for parents about their *family:*

❏ What are the dynamics within your family? Do you have other family members (siblings, spouses, parents) that require attention and time? Remember, only one parent and the child may attend auditions and shooting, so you may need to make arrangements for babysitting, meals, and other family activities to fit around audition and shooting schedules.

❏ Does your child get on with his or her siblings, or is there any sibling rivalry?

❏ Do you want to involve more than one child?

❏ Do all your children have good relationships with both parents?

❏ Are you financially stable? While it's true that some children have earned enough money from film and television to put them through a college education, if your motives are purely financial, you can end up putting undue pressure on your child and yourself to succeed, which can be a sure path to failure.

2
ASSEMBLING YOUR TEAM

Do I need an agent?

The days of being "discovered" on the street are gone. If you want to work in the film or television industry, you need an agent. Wherever I have spoken to audiences on children in show business, the topic of agents is a hot one:

☆ They want money up front!

☆ They said my six-year-old has to take classes!

☆ How do I get one?

☆ Whom do I trust?

☆ What can they charge me for?

Some talent agencies are good, honest, and successful. Unfortunately, many are bad. Trust your instincts when choosing an agent for your child. You will have to work closely with the agent and should have a good working relationship with him or her. Remember that you may be working with an agent for many years, so you should like him or her, and feel good about dealing with the agency.

Not all agents can be all things. It is common to have one agent for background work, one agent for voice work, and another for principal or commercial work. Larger agencies may have different departments that handle different types of work. If you have a different agent for each type of work, be sure to tell each agent about any other agent you may have.

Many parents feel that a personal rapport with the agent is the most important thing to consider when choosing one. Others look at it in strictly a business sense, not really caring whether they like the agent personally as long as he or she gets the job done. The decision is up to you.

How are agents paid?

The laws that govern talent agencies vary in their wording from place to place, but the spirit of the law stays the same. Legitimate agencies make their money through commission on income earned.

In the United States, the Screen Actors Guild (SAG) signatory agreements limit the percentage commission that agents can take to 10 percent of the gross earnings of your child.

In Canada, an agent can take up to 15 percent of the gross earnings of your child. In Ontario, the agency can charge you a monthly fee for office expenses. In British Columbia, an agent can charge you $25 for taking a photo of your child but the cost has to be deducted from monies earned.

Each state and province has different rules about what amounts can be deducted, so make sure you find out at your initial interview with a prospective agent exactly what he or she charges.

The percentage the agent takes from the work of the performer is the only money an agent should take. Talent agencies are not specially regulated for minors, and percentages are the same for adults as they are for children.

Even though the laws governing agency commissions are basic in their structure, many people still lose money simply because they don't know what the law allows. The glamor of show business, combined with the beauty of our children, is a powerful lure. According to the Better Business Bureau, modeling/talent agency scams are the fastest growing category of scams in North America.

Knowledge is your best defense. If you follow the guidelines in this chapter for finding an agent, you should have the knowledge to avoid getting taken for your hard earned money.

Use Checklist 2 when interviewing agents to make sure you get answers to all your questions.

How do I find an agent?

Your quest for an agency to represent your child begins on the telephone. Your local union office (SAG or ACTRA) will have the best listing for talent agents. Sit down with the list and start making telephone calls. You can also send a letter to prospective agents (see Sample 1).

The best agents are busy people, and often you cannot speak to the agent directly. This is good because you hope the agent will be busy with your child. The person who answers the telephone is usually helpful and will tell you what he or she can. Agencies field hundreds of inquiries every day from people wanting representation. Be brief, and simply ask if the agency is accepting new talent at this time and if they want your child's photograph and resume.

Some agencies do not handle children. Some may have a full roster of seven-year-old girls. By calling, it will save you and the agency time and money. Agencies that state they are not accepting new talent, are not, and do not want to get your child's photo. Save your time and money — don't send one. If the agency requests a short, two- or three-minute videotape of your child, you may want to produce a short tape of your child telling a joke or singing a song.

When choosing an agent, decide whether location is an issue for you. Sometimes an agent may ask you to bring in your child and will want to meet both of you without sending in a photo. However, once your child has an agent, most business is carried out by telephone, fax, or e-mail, so there isn't a lot of need to go into the agent's office.

Don't be impressed or fooled by the agent's office. The agent may have a big fancy office, but big and fancy doesn't necessarily mean it is a legitimate agency. In many places, an agency can be operated as a home-based business. Consult your notes on the agencies you have visited before you make a decision. Try not to decide on the spot in the agent's office.

Agents deduct their commission from income your child has earned. You should pay no money up front.

CHECKLIST 2
QUESTIONS TO ASK AN AGENCY

When you are interviewing prospective agents, you may want to ask them some or all of the following questions:

❑ What are some of the projects your clients have worked on?

❑ Do you do background booking?

❑ How many children like mine (same age/gender/coloring) are on your roster?

❑ Can I talk to parents of other children represented by the agency?

❑ Do you have children that are full or apprentice members of the industry unions? (See Chapter 9.)

❑ Do you belong to a breakdown service?

❑ Do you suggest registering with an Internet breakdown service?

❑ How do you work your payment system?

❑ How long have you been a talent agent and how long has the agency been in business?

❑ Do you have contacts outside the area (e.g., Toronto, Los Angeles, Vancouver, New York)?

❑ What is your standard business contract?

❑ What is your contract cancellation policy?

Listen carefully to the answer and don't be afraid to take notes. Some things that indicate it might be the wrong agency:

❑ What's a breakdown service?

❑ What's the Internet?

❑ We require a small deposit.

❑ Our photographer will be available today.

❑ I guarantee that I can get your child work, if he or she takes these classes, uses this photographer …

❑ The agency doesn't want to meet your child, but will represent the child without seeing him or her. (The exception to this is if your are looking for representation for an infant. In that case, be sure to ask how many infants the agency has on its roster.)

CHECKLIST 2 — CONTINUED

❑ A hundred of the photos of the clients look just like your child.

❑ If there is a bank machine in the office, run away.

After you have made your telephone calls, gather your information together and send the agents, who were interested in your child, your package. This should include the following:

☆ **A photograph.** Send the same photograph to everyone. The photograph you send must be a good clean shot of your child's face. If your child is of school age, the school photo is usually suitable. Try to choose one where there aren't any shadows blocking the eyes or where the face is large enough to see clearly. If your child is under school age, a retail studio-type photo could be good. If you have a digital camera and the technological know-how, ask if you can submit a photo by e-mail. See Chapter 4 for a detailed discussion of professional photos.

☆ **Resume.** You may ask yourself, how do I write a resume for my six-month-old? Actually, a resume when your child starts is for statistical information. It should include height, weight, hair and eye color, clothes size, and shoe size. It doesn't have to be in any fancy format; just make sure it is neat and legible. For older children, be sure to include any special skills they have. If they are taking martial arts, list what belt or level they have mastered. If they take piano, say how long they have been taking lessons. Skiing, snowboarding, skateboarding, or anything your child likes to do and is fairly proficient at is a skill. Don't lie or exaggerate. It is very embarrassing for both your child and agent to be suggested for a part that requires a special skill that your child doesn't have. See Sample 2 for an example of a resume.

☆ **Your contact information, telephone numbers, and address.** Be sure to include your contact information on both the resume and photograph. You would be surprised at how many photographs agents receive that have no way for the agent to contact the parents.

SAMPLE 1
LETTER TO AGENT

Mary Smith
123 Star Avenue
Smithville, USA
55555

15 October 200-

Joe Smith
Smith Talent Agency
123 Agent Street
Smithville, USA
55555

Dear Sir/Madam,

Enclosed is a photo and resume for my child, Jane Smith. She is a bright, outgoing child, and I believe she will do well in this industry.

I am aware of the time commitment it takes to be involved in this industry, and I have the means and am available to travel to auditions and shooting.

I can be contacted at my workplace during office hours at 222-555-9999 or at home after hours at 222-555-7777. Please feel free to leave me a message.

I look forward to hearing from you.

Sincerely,

Mary Smith

Mary Smith

SAMPLE 2
RESUME

Date: 15 October 200-

Child's name: Jane Smith

Child's date of birth: 15 May 199-

Weight: 80 lbs

Hair color: Light brown

Eye color: Light brown

Skintone or ethnicity: Caucasian

Talents:

[Put down what your child can do, for example:

Infant: Able to crawl on all fours, can walk, can sit unaided, can drink from a glass, doesn't make shy.

Two-year-old: Child has a good vocabulary, can skip, likes to be photographed.

School aged: Involved in karate, swimming, dance for ___ years.]

Contact: Mary Smith
            123 Star Avenue
            Smithville, USA
            55555
            Tel: 222-555-7777 or 222-555-9999

If you enclose a stamped, self-addressed envelope with your package, it may help you to get an answer sooner.

Don't try to get answers to your questions on the telephone; save the questions for the interview. Some agents may respond to an e-mail if you call and ask first.

Use Worksheet 1 to keep track of the agencies you have contacted and which ones you have sent packages. Record the date that you sent out the package. How many packages you send out depends on you. The more agents you talk to, the more educated a decision you can make when selecting one.

How long does it take for an agent to get back to you? You should give it a couple of weeks. If you haven't heard from anyone after a few weeks, then go back to your agent contact list and call those agents you sent a package. Tell them this is a follow-up call to confirm that they have received your package. Agents will probably not get in touch with you if they do not wish to handle your child.

Unless your child is an infant, most agencies will not take on your child by just looking at the photo. They will call you in for an interview. When you go in to meet with an agent, be prepared with the questions you want answered. Any concern you have is a good question. Don't consider anything you have to ask as trivial. See Checklist 2 for some questions you may want to ask the agent.

Choosing a good agent

Before you set any appointments with an agent, do a little research yourself about the agencies. Call the Better Business Bureau and inquire about any consumer complaints.

One way to know whether you are dealing with a legitimate talent agency is to check the agency's standing within the industry's professional association. Talent agencies belong to a couple of different organizations. In Canada, the Talent Agents and Managers Association of Canada (TAMAC) members are recognized as legitimate professionals within the entertainment industry. In the United States, there are two major talent associations: The Association of Talent Agents (ATA) and the National Association of Talent Representatives (NATR). You can find the local contact details for any of these organizations in your telephone book. Check out the Appendix for ATA and NATR's Web site addresses.

Performers' unions will also be able to help you establish the legitimacy of an agent. In the United States, agents that are independent of either the Association of Talent Agents (ATA) or the National Association of Talent Representatives (NATR) are regulated and franchised by the Screen Actors Guild (SAG). There used

WORKSHEET 1
AGENCY TRACKING

Agency:	Stars in Your Eyes Talent
Telephone number:	303-555-7878
Person talked to:	Irving Script
Accepting talent:	yes __X__ no_____
Sent package:	yes __X__ no_____
Mailing address:	456 Hollywood Blvd, Los Angeles
Notes to myself:	Mr. Script was very pleasant to talk to.
Date sent:	15 October 200- Follow-up date: 3 December 200-
Follow-up activity:	(e.g., got a reply, booked an interview, or was declined)

Agency:	
Telephone number:	
Person talked to:	
Accepting talent:	yes _____ no_____
Sent package:	yes _____ no_____
Mailing address:	
Notes to myself:	
Date sent:	Follow-up date:
Follow-up activity:	

Agency:	
Telephone number:	
Person talked to:	
Accepting talent:	yes _____ no_____
Sent package:	yes _____ no_____
Mailing address:	
Notes to myself:	
Date sent:	Follow-up date:
Follow-up activity:	

WORKSHEET 1 — CONTINUED

Agency:	
Telephone number:	
Person talked to:	
Accepting talent:	yes _____ no _____
Sent package:	yes _____ no _____
Mailing address:	
Notes to myself:	
Date sent:	Follow-up date:
Follow-up activity:	

Agency:	
Telephone number:	
Person talked to:	
Accepting talent:	yes _____ no _____
Sent package:	yes _____ no _____
Mailing address:	
Notes to myself:	
Date sent:	Follow-up date:
Follow-up activity:	

Agency:	
Telephone number:	
Person talked to:	
Accepting talent:	yes _____ no _____
Sent package:	yes _____ no _____
Mailing address:	
Notes to myself:	
Date sent:	Follow-up date:
Follow-up activity:	

to be a SAG rule that required actors to use a franchised agency, but that rule has been suspended. There is currently no agreement between SAG, and ATA and NATR. This means that SAG members can now be represented by an agency that is a member of either ATA or NATR. This is important because, after doing one SAG job in the United States, you must join that union.

In Canada, there is no agreement between the Alliance of Canadian Cinema, Television, and Radio Artists (ACTRA) and talent agencies, but the offices of ACTRA will tell you if an agent is in good standing with the union.

See Chapter 9 for more information on unions.

Getting agents to come to you

If what has been described above sounds like more than you are prepared to do to find an agent, you could try having an agent come to you.

The Casting Workbook <www.castingworkbook.com> is an actor/agent Internet service. You can list your child in the "unrepresented" category, called the Talent Scout, and see if an agent will call you. Some great agent/client relationships have started this way. The Casting Workbook is widely used by casting directors and agents throughout North America, Australia, and other parts of the world.

There are thousands of other Web sites that offer you a chance to list your child on a database for casting directors to look at. Some charge fees of hundreds of dollars, while others are free. Be very careful with these services. Unless you are sure that only reputable casting people have access to the database, don't use the service. If you can access the roster without being an agent or without a special password, then don't use the service. Be aware of the safety risks on the Internet.

What if I live out of town?

In some smaller cities, your choice of agents may be very limited. Very small markets may not even have talent agents. There are still avenues you can take to get your child involved in the entertainment industry. Take your child's photograph and resume to

In New York and Los Angeles there is a book available at drama shops called the Ross REPORTS. This book lists all the agents in these two cities. In Toronto, Theatre Ontario publishes an AGENTS BOOK that lists Ontario agents.

Bear in mind that any traveling costs to auditions is your responsibility.

the production people at your local television station. Often they produce local commercials or programming. Local radio stations may like to have a tape of your child doing voices. Commercials are always being taped at local radio stations. This is a good way to start. If your child is successful doing local work, look at working your way up the ladder by sending a photo and resume to the next larger market.

Choosing the right agent for your child is probably the most important decision you will have to make in this industry. It is also your first success in show business. You will not get an answer from every agent you send a photo. Not all agencies you interview will want to handle your child. So regard signing up your child with an agent as the first success of hopefully many. Not everybody can make it that far.

Do I need a manager?

There is a trend in the film and television industry for parents to hire a manager or talent consultant for children. I do not recommend you do this if your child is just starting out. Very often, these agencies take your money up front for the promise of work or guidance.

If your child becomes successful, a business manager for handling your finances is a great addition to your team, and a personal manager may also be useful. However, I recommend you consider these people only when your child's success surpasses the abilities of you and your agent.

Should my child take classes?

Some classes for children in the five-to-seven-year age group are play and confidence classes, which can be helpful for building your child's confidence. What you don't want, however, is a child that is going to look and act coached.

Beware of agents who tell you that your child needs to take a specific class from a specific place before being sent on an audition. Very often they just want your money. Classes for very young children are seldom a good idea. If your child has attended some auditions and your agent gets feedback suggesting that lessons might be needed, you may want to consider what classes are available to legitimately help your child. But any suggestion for classes should only come once the agent has had a chance to get to know your child's potential or weaknesses.

The choice of classes is always yours. In many areas, the law forbids a talent agency from also running an acting school. I suggest you check out for yourself any classes that have been recommended. Talk to other parents of children who have been through them and then decide what class (if any) is right for your child.

Talent and model searches

Every few months, a company may come to your city and advertise a talent and model search. The company will flood the city and surrounding areas with slick advertising aimed at teenagers and young parents. What it offers you is a chance to be seen by a number of agents and sometimes casting directors. What it sells you is a package to a convention.

At the initial search, hundreds of people will wait hours to be seen by a panel of judges. If your child is chosen by the panel, you will be taken into another area where you will be presented with a opportunity to attend the convention. This convention will cost a minimum of several hundred dollars. At the convention, you will be offered modeling classes, photo sessions, and acting classes for your child. The price to attend the convention does not include the cost of enrolling your child in the classes or photo sessions offered.

There is a chance your child will be seen by an agent. Some people with agents attend these searches hoping to have their child "discovered," or to receive a better opportunity than they already have.

Some talent agency regulations do not explicitly prohibit a talent agency from operating a modeling school. Be aware of what type of agency you are signing up with. The modeling and print industries are unregulated and often filled with empty promises and pitfalls.

3
THE CASTING CALL

The actors who play the characters in a film or commercial can often make or break the production. In some productions, scripts may be written with a particular actor in mind, but most often actors will need to audition for a part.

Directors usually have specific ideas about the kind of actor they are looking for to portray a character. Before auditions are even held, potential actors are eliminated from the process simply because they do not fit the profile of the part. For example, they may be too young, too good-looking, or too tall. Some actors can be molded to fit the part, and directors have been known to change the scope of a part in order to cast a particular actor. For example, an American actor can learn to speak with a British accent. Or a 30-year-old can be made to look like a 70-year-old with the help of prosthetics and makeup.

But if the part calls for an African-American boy living in Chicago and his ethnicity is central to the role, don't waste everybody's time by insisting to your agent that your blue-eyed, blond-haired boy be allowed to audition. While you want to put your child in front of as many casting directors as you can, try to recognize the limits (as well as the potential) of your child and the suitability of available roles.

How does casting work?

Casting is the process of auditioning, selecting, or suggesting the right child for the part in a production. This is the job of casting directors (often called CDs), who are hired by advertising agencies or production houses. Over time, you will become familiar with the casting directors in your area. Some work exclusively with children, some do only television work, and some have only movie contracts.

When casting directors know there are a lot of projects coming up, they will prescreen actors so that they have a list of names ready for upcoming auditions. This process is called a *nonspecific prescreen*.

If your child receives positive feedback from these prescreens, he or she is on that casting director's "A list"! This means that the casting director has had a chance to look at your child and will keep him or her in mind for upcoming projects.

Diagram 1 shows the process you and your child will go through to be cast in a production.

How do they decide who will audition?

To find the right child for a part, the casting director first has to know what the part is. The producer or director will give the casting director specifications for the part. The production may require a specific ethnicity, height, hair, and eye color. Or it may require a specific skill (such as the ability to balance a basketball on one finger). Infants may be required to hold a bottle or crawl to a toy and pick it up.

As your child goes on auditions, you will get to know what casting directors are seeing in him or her. An agent can push for your child to be seen for a large part, but don't expect it to happen often. It certainly won't happen for toy or diaper commercials.

When the casting director knows what he or she is looking for, the CD will release a breakdown to the talent agencies. The breakdown is a description of the character or the "look" the production is searching for.

DIAGRAM 1
THE ROAD TO STARDOM

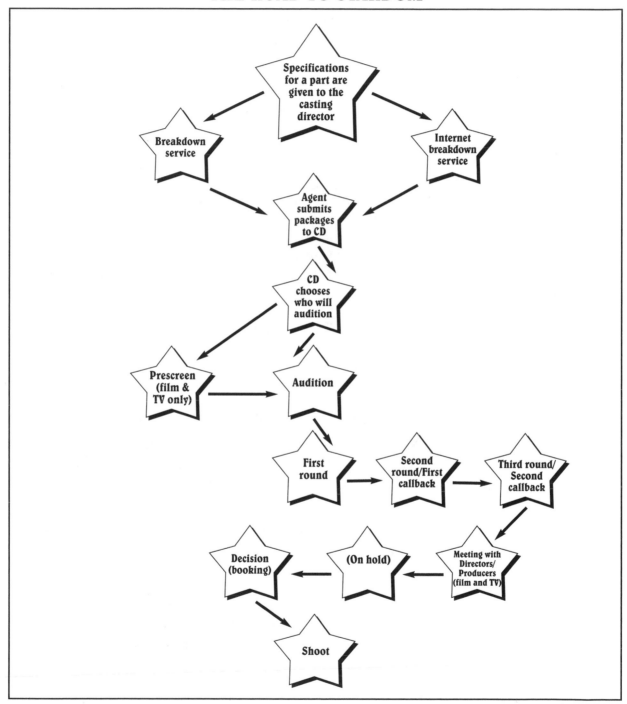

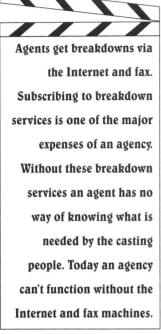

Breakdown services

In large markets, breakdown services make available the breakdowns for that day. An agent will compile a package consisting of the headshots and resumes of actors that are suitable for the part. At a certain time each day, the breakdown service picks up the package for delivery to the casting director. The casting director then looks at all the headshots from the different agencies and selects who will audition.

All agencies use some sort of breakdown service, and theoretically the casting director will look at all the submissions. Any agency can submit for a project. In reality, however, the casting director may only look at the packages from certain agencies and fill the audition spots from those packages. A casting director may know that certain agencies have good ethnic children, some agencies have new talent, and some agencies have experienced talent. As you can imagine, your agency's relationship with the casting directors is very important. This is one of those "behind the scenes" situations you have no control over. You have to trust that your agency will look after the interest of your child by suggesting him or her for every suitable part. Of course, as your child becomes known to the casting directors, they can often request to see your child for a particular audition. See Chapter 2 for more information on choosing an agency.

Internet breakdown services

Many casting directors use Internet breakdown services to select the children they want to see for a part. Casting directors can input their criteria (e.g., hair color and age) and the search engine on the Web site will generate the names of children registered on the database who match that description. The casting directors can then contact the agents of the children they want to see.

When you sign up with an agency, they should tell you to join an Internet breakdown service. You pay the yearly fee directly to the service and your child's photo and vital statistics are posted. Internet breakdown services can broaden the exposure and opportunity for your child (especially if you don't live near a major city) as many casting directors all over the world look for talent on a global scale.

The largest and most widely used Internet breakdown service in the industry is called The Casting Workbook <www.casting-workbook.com>. Be very careful if you consider using any other Internet service. They claim they are used by many casting directors and will charge you for being listed. Do not sign anything until you get an agent — unless you are using the talent scout section. There are new sites on the Internet everyday, making it almost impossible to track them or keep up with them. Your safest bet is to discuss it with your agent or check the site with your local union.

Auditions

After the casting director has determined what talent he or she will see, the agents are contacted and times are set for auditions. If your child is lucky enough to be considered, your agent will call you with the audition time.

Casting can take a number of steps. Hundreds of children may be seen at the first round of auditions, especially for diaper commercials or for productions involving younger children.

At the second round of auditions or the first callback, the field is narrowed. Only one-tenth of the original children may be seen. If the product requires a special setting or a special skill, a third round or second callback may be held. At this stage the child will usually have to perform that special skill, such as rollerblade or swim.

Second callbacks are often held in a different place than the original audition.

Who will be at the audition?

The first audition may only involve the casting director and a camera operator. Sometimes the casting director's assistant may conduct the first round. If this happens, the casting director will review the tape of the children and determine who will be seen for the callback. Tapes can be made in any city and sent to the casting director's office for viewing. It is not unusual to audition in Vancouver for a commercial to be shot in New York or audition in Kansas City for a commercial to be shot in Toronto.

During a callback, executives from the advertising agency or production house, representatives for the product, or the director of the commercial may also attend.

How do directors decide which child to use?

The director will usually decide which child to use after the call-backs. As with everything else in this business, the usual can always change. Your child may be brought in for the callback round without having done the first audition. The people that make the casting decision may not like any of the choices and may start the whole process over again with a whole new batch of kids. Or they may decide to change what they are looking for. They may decide to go with an older or younger group of children. They may cast the commercial and then scrap the whole project at the last minute.

Often, when you see 30 children that look the same at an audition, you may think to yourself, how will they choose a child when they all seem so much alike? A major component of casting is how well a child reacts to strangers, or, in older children, how well the child can take direction. If a child is too cute, he or she will outshine the product and people will remember the child and not the product. Or a child may not be cute enough! Save yourself some stress and don't try to second-guess the casting directors. You just never know what they see that makes them pick one child over another.

One of the biggest disappointments for you as a parent is seeing the finished project that your child auditioned for and knowing in your heart that your child could have done that. Bear in mind that your child does have something the directors were looking for, otherwise he or she would not have been seen in the first place.

Who decides who gets the part?

The final decision as to who actually gets the part may be made by a number of people. For commercials, it is rarely the actual casting director. More than likely the advertising agency that designed the commercial will make the final decision. When casting young children or infants, the advertising agency may film all the suggestions from the casting director and then make a final decision during the final editing.

For small actor roles in film and television, the director and maybe the producer may want to see only one or two suggestions for the part. In that case, the casting director will narrow down the suggestion to the required number.

For larger roles, the director and producer will work together to see the candidates. They may want to see only a limited number of actors, so the casting directors have to know their jobs in order to suggest just the right people.

Knowing that the casting director may not have a final say in the actual job doesn't prevent a lot of sour grapes being squashed. You may hear stories from parents complaining that a child got the part because he or she is related to or knows the casting director. Don't let this spoil your attitude; it is usually not the case.

Why is more than one child often hired?

When casting young children under the age of three, more than one child is hired. For a diaper commercial as many as 20 babies may be hired. Some will be used for their faces, their cute bottoms, their walk, or even their hands. Extra babies will be hired to be used in case the first choice doesn't work out on the day of shooting.

How does casting differ for film and television?

For film and television casting, depending on the size of the role, a prescreen may be held before the actual audition. At a prescreen your child may have to read lines with a casting director. Prescreens are not usually taped and usually just the casting director attends. If the casting director thinks your child can handle the role, then an audition will be held.

Casting directors look at far fewer children for film and television projects than for commercials. Experience plays a part in determining who will audition, but children with no previous experience still have a chance.

The audition is taped and reviewed. Often your child may be called back for another look. At the callback for film and television, the director and sometimes the producer can be there. For leads and major parts, there can be any number of callbacks and meetings with the director before the final decision is made.

The process of getting the lines to read at the actual audition is called a cold read. Your child will be required to read the lines without having seen them before. As your child gets older and more experienced, the ability to do a cold read is very important as it demonstrates his or her ability to interpret a part.

Taping auditions

Taping an audition to be sent away is becoming common practice. A casting director may notice your child on The Casting Work-book and want to see him or her. Your agent will tell you if a self-taped audition or a studio-taped audition is required.

For a self-taped audition, you will need to produce a home video of your child doing whatever is needed. If you need a studio tape, your agent will arrange for studio time and professional lighting and camera work.

The tapes are then sent to the casting director. If the director wants to see you, he or she will either come to you in person or arrange to have you come to him or her. From there, the callback process is the same as described above.

On hold

Between the final callback and actually booking your child for a part, your child may be put on hold or first refusal. These are courtesy terms only and have no contractual obligations. Often your agent may not even tell you if your child is on hold.

Casting background

For film and sometimes television, a separate casting director may cast for background actors. The background casting director will see to it that the people who are hired match the setting of the shoot. If the shot is in a museum, the background casting director will ensure that the background actors look like patrons of the arts. If the scene requires homeless people, the background casting director ensures that the same patrons of the arts are not lounging in the streets.

Background casting directors have the resources to make hundreds of background performers available. Generally, auditions are not held for background work. The background casting director will contact agencies and tell them to send out specific people or characters.

Continuity background work could require a "look see" where the director will take a look at the people the background casting director wants to use. The director may or may not use any or all of the people that are suggested. See Chapter 6 for more information on working background.

Internet message boards

The Internet has become a double-edged sword for agents. On the positive side, the Internet allows agents to submit talent electronically to casting agents. However, the down side for agents is the proliferation of public message boards that have sprung up in the last few years.

Public message boards allow people to post messages about any topic and read the replies from other people. They are usually discussions about the film and television business, agents, and auditions. Most of these message boards are started and maintained by parents of children in the business, but some are set up by professionals, managers, or agents. Much of the information on these boards can be good and right. However, they can also lead you on the wrong path.

Some message boards post information about auditions. If you see an audition posted that you think is suitable for your child, use your discretion before calling your agent and demanding that your child go on the audition. Remember what you have read so far. You have to develop a rapport with your agent. You should have faith that your agent is submitting your child for all the projects that your child has a chance at. By the same token, if you are reading about a whole lot of auditions that your child isn't going on, then maybe you need to call your agent. It is hard not to feel your child should be going on all those auditions.

Some of the message boards are started to get business. Message boards or chat rooms have been set up by management or agencies simply as a way of advertising their companies and acquiring paying customers.

Because there is no way to control who posts what on these boards, treat them with a grain of salt and with caution. Be aware of who started the board and who sponsors it.

4
HEADSHOTS

The 8-by-10-inch glossy is one of the long-standing traditions of Hollywood that hasn't changed. These professional photographs are called *headshots*. Sooner or later you are going to need them, although there is long-standing debate about just how soon. You don't need to send headshots to agents when you are trying to find representation. Although photographers can work with quite young children, many agents discourage getting headshots for young children because children can change quickly over a short period of time. Some parents like to get headshots because of the quality of photographs. It is a financial call you will have to make. If you can afford them, and if nothing becomes of your child's career, then you still have some good photographs of your child.

How important is a good headshot?

A headshot is the first look a casting director gets of your child. The first glance a casting director gives the photograph lasts a fraction of a second; if he or she is looking on the Internet, that glance will last a fraction longer. It is not a lot of time. When a casting director is looking at headshots, he or she knows what to look for and can spot it quickly. If your child's photo is radically different from the standard, a casting director could look right past it. Make the casting director's job easier (and improve your child's chances of being picked) by sticking to the headshot formula used in the industry.

What to send out for your agent search

Carefully choose a photograph to send to prospective agents. Eighty percent of the photograph should be of your child's face, and the face should be large enough that you can tell the child's eye color and hair color. A natural smile will show your child's best attributes. If your child is school age, often the photos taken at school will be suitable for sending to an agent. Photos taken at a retail photo studio can also be suitable. Send the same photo to all the agents you contact. Use a very recent photo, especially if your child is under two.

Taking your own headshots

If you want to take your child's headshots yourself, use true black-and-white film. Take the shots outdoors on a light cloudy day. Avoid taking shots in the bright sunlight because it is almost impossible not to squint. Choose a location where there is nothing noticeable in the background. You should be able to adjust your depth of field so that only your child's face is in focus. Watch carefully for where shadows are falling as you don't want any on the face.

You can also take the headshots indoors using a plain wall as the background. Don't be afraid to get close with the camera; remember, you want the whole frame to be filled with your child's face. When you look at the photographs you have taken, be very critical of them. Take them to your agent's office, ask his or her opinion, and compare them to professional shots.

Choosing a photographer

The choices for a photographer can be astounding, especially in larger centers such as Los Angeles and New York. Prices can vary from under a hundred dollars to well over three hundred.

The style of each photographer can affect the look of your child's headshots. If you have found an agent, ask for advice.

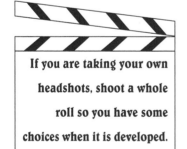

If you are taking your own headshots, shoot a whole roll so you have some choices when it is developed. Don't assume that two or three shots are all you are going to need.

Agents can recommend a photographer and show you some of the work done for their other clients. Remember, though, that a talent agent should not make you use a specific photographer. You should have the choice yourself.

You should see the work of a couple of the photographers your agent recommends. Make an appointment to go to their studios, or, if they have a Web site, then look there. Ask your agent if you can call a parent that has used that photographer. You want to know how that child did with that photographer. You may hear responses such as, the photographer was patient or impatient, he or she was late for the sitting, or we felt comfortable and unhurried. Sometimes taking your child with you to look at the photographer's work will give you a good idea of whom you should hire to do the headshots. If your child plays shy or doesn't communicate with the photographer, you should probably look elsewhere. If the cost and quality are relatively level, go with your instincts when choosing a photographer.

Preparing for the photo shoot

Once you have decided on the photographer, you need to prepare for the photo shoot. Most important, make the appointment for the time you know your child is at his or her best. If your child is a chipper morning bird, take advantage of that. A child's moods show up clearly in a photo. Don't make an appointment during nap time, or try to squeeze it in between school and soccer practice.

Make sure your child is well rested and doesn't have any visible injuries from the playground or sports practice. Some small scrapes and faint dark circles under the eyes can be covered with makeup.

You may want to bring a change of clothes. One shirt with a collar and one without can give you two very different looks. If your daughter has long hair, you may want one photograph with her hair down and one with her hair pinned up.

Remember, the casting director expects your child to show up at the audition looking like the headshots. If you're going to spend hours curling your daughter's hair for her photo session, be prepared to do the same thing for auditions.

Don't use an agent who insists you use his or her photographer. This is an old scam of getting your money through an expensive in-house photographer and then never sending your child on an audition.

Darker clothing works well, and avoid loud colors and patterns. Don't use any clothing that has a visible logo or emblem. When you make the appointment, ask the photographer what he or she recommends.

Most headshots are done in the studio with a plain backdrop, but some photographers prefer to work outdoors in natural light. You may want to find a quiet spot out of sight from your child to watch your child's photo shoot. Do not leave the room completely; you should always be able to see what your child is doing.

If you are having photographs taken of siblings, it might be easier on them if you do it on two separate days, taking them individually to the studio. Photographers usually allow a couple of hours per shoot. The advantage of taking them on the same day, however, is that you might want to get some photographs taken of your children together, although those photographs will not be professionally used.

Getting headshots done is work. If your child is old enough to take direction, then the photographer will tell your child how to tilt his or her head or lean into the shot. Try it for yourself! Smiling for a camera can be difficult. A headshot session is a good feeler for working on camera. A relaxed, comfortable child will show in the photos, and casting directors and agents can see that.

Choosing the headshot

The turnaround time between having the shoot done and getting the photographs can be as little as 24 hours. You and your agent will have to decide which photo to get enlarged and use in submission packages and to take to auditions.

Some photographers provide contact sheets as a proof. If you are looking at a contact sheet, you will need a magnifying glass or loop to see the shots clearly.

Other photographers provide 4-by-6-inch proofs. The best way to select from 4-by-6-inch proofs is to lay them all out on a table. Eliminate any that have the eyes closed, or too much shadow. Leave the rest out on the table for a couple of days. As you walk by them, choose one or two to set aside. Look at the others and set aside another that you like. Put your choices back on the table with the rest. Keep doing that and the one that you like the most will keep being put aside.

Don't use any props for the photo. Your child may look cute holding a teddy bear in a photo for grandma, but not for a casting director. Under the age of about four it is all right to have your child's hands in the photo, but for older children you want only the head and shoulders.

Sample 3: Contact Sheet (two-year-old) shows how two different shirts change the photograph dramatically. You can see the photos that can be eliminated right off the bat. The shots with eyes closed, pressed lips, and forced smiles will not work. The child was just over two when the photos were taken, and you can see how many shots you may need to take of a youngster to result in some choices that will work. The choice for enlargement was based on the clarity of the child's face and the contrast of the two different looks (see Sample 4).

In Sample 5, the child is now four. It is almost more difficult to keep a four-year-old focused than a two-year-old in order to get good shots. The photographer let the child loosen up by taking some "silly shots." Again, two different looks were achieved with two different hairstyles. The enlargement was chosen because of the natural look of the child, the clarity of the face, and the long hair is noticeable over the shoulder, so casting directors can see it (see Sample 6).

Sample 7 shows an older child. An older child should be able to take direction and stay focused so that the photographer can get many good shots. You can see how much of the original photograph gets cropped so that only the head and shoulders of the child are used in the enlargement (see Sample 8.)

The five shots on the left column of Sample 9 show some examples of bad lighting. These shots also use bad backgrounds; the horizontal line makes it look like a stick is growing out of the child's head. Also, some use of shadow makes the child look slimmer (although an agent would not use these photos because a casting director would expect to see a slimmer child).

Making reproductions

Part of a headshot package is usually one or two enlargements. One is usually the photographer's choice and one is your choice. After you have your 8-by-10-inch photograph, it is usually your responsibility to get copies made. You have to take them to a reprographics house to be done. Check in your Yellow Pages for reprographics houses near you, or ask your agent for a recommendation. Reprographic copies are done on photographic paper so the thickness and glossiness is the same as the original. A larger

SAMPLE 3
CONTACT SHEET (TWO-YEAR-OLD)

SAMPLE 4
ENLARGEMENT (WITH INSERT)

SAMPLE 5
CONTACT SHEET (FOUR-YEAR-OLD)

SAMPLE 6
ENLARGEMENT (FOUR-YEAR-OLD)

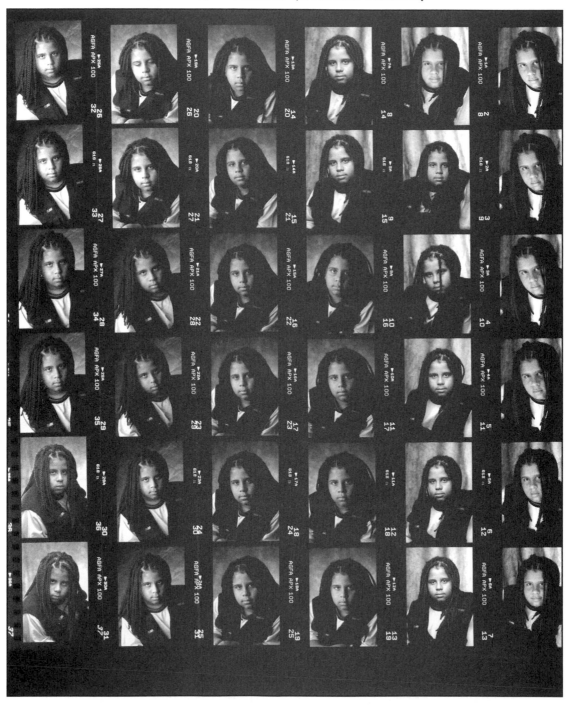

SAMPLE 8
ENLARGEMENT (OLDER CHILD)

SAMPLE 9
CONTACT SHEET WITH BAD LIGHTING

negative is made so the quality of the copy exactly matches the original. Don't try to make copies on a Xerox machine — it looks really bad.

Some agencies have their logo on file at the reprographic house so that when you get your copies made, they have the agency's logo on the bottom (or on the back) of the photo. Some agencies do not require their logo to be on the photograph. Check what your agency's requirements are. The child's name is always clearly printed on the reproductions.

Reproductions involve a small set-up fee and can run anywhere from 40 cents a copy to $2 each, often depending on the quantity you order.

Some photographers offer to reprint photos from the computer onto photo paper so that they look and feel close to reproductions. The cost for setup is higher than standard reproductions, but the cost per reproduction is close. Many photographers are using computer software to create interesting headshots. They may use interesting lettering, inserts (smaller pictures along side the larger one), and different borders. The industry standard is a single shot 8-by-10-inch glossy, but an insert to show a child's different looks is becoming accepted. See Sample 4 for an example.

Your agent will let you know how many copies he or she needs to start off with. Some agents will send a shot to all the casting directors in your area for their files. You will need enough copies to take to auditions, and to send to whatever online casting service your agent uses. And of course you will need one for the grandparents and for you to have in your home or office.

Black and white is still the preferred choice for headshots because it hides most skin flaws and will scan and fax better than color.

5
THE AUDITION

Your agent calls! Your child is off to his or her first audition. It is pretty exciting. You and your child may be nervous, but the more auditions you go to, the more familiar you will become with the procedure. This chapter provides advice to help you stay organized when attending auditions, as well as some tips for making the audition process go smoothly.

Keeping track of the details

With a bit of luck this won't be the only audition your child will go to. Keeping track of the details of auditions can sometimes be bewildering, but if you stay organized, you can make the audition process smooth and stress free. Use the audition tracking form (see Worksheet 2) to help you keep organized. We will use the form to walk through the auditioning process.

Who goes to the audition?

If you have three sons, Tom, Dick, and Harry, you need to use this space. It is not unusual for more than one member of the family to be in the business.

WORKSHEET 2
AUDITION TRACKING FORM

Who:	
Day/date:	
Time:	
Place:	
Casting director:	
Project:	
Scene:	
Appearance:	
Lines:	No Yes Attached There
Callback date:	
Shoot date:	
Expenses:	
Got callback?	

Who:	
Day/date:	
Time:	
Place:	
Casting director:	
Project:	
Scene:	
Appearance:	
Lines:	No Yes Attached There
Callback date:	
Shoot date:	
Expenses:	
Got callback?	

Who:	
Day/date:	
Time:	
Place:	
Casting director:	
Project:	
Scene:	
Appearance:	
Lines:	No Yes Attached There
Callback date:	
Shoot date:	
Expenses:	
Got callback?	

Who:	
Day/date:	
Time:	
Place:	
Casting director:	
Project:	
Scene:	
Appearance:	
Lines:	No Yes Attached There
Callback date:	
Shoot date:	
Expenses:	
Got callback?	

Day/date

Write down both the day and the date of the audition. The lead time for auditions is usually about two or three days, and getting a call the day before an audition is standard practice. However, getting a call at 11:00 at night the day before an audition is not. If this happens, you should check that your agent is giving you the information as soon as he or she is getting it, and if not, ask why. Getting a call the day of the audition is rare, but can happen, especially if the casting director wants to see your child specifically.

Time

When you have an audition time of 1:00 p.m., don't make an appointment with Aunt Mary for tea at 2:00 p.m. Auditioning can sometimes be a quick process, but it can also be painfully slow. Try to arrive at the audition about 15 minutes before time — but don't show up an hour ahead of time expecting to get out sooner! Auditions can be set up by the casting director to see specific children together. They may be grouped by gender, size, or age. So if you show up at noon, they may still be seeing eight-year-old girls when you have a nine-year-old boy, and you will be waiting an hour.

If you have an important appointment previously scheduled for the same time you are to go on an audition, talk to your agent first. Sometimes agents are given a block of time that they fill with their clients. You may have a little working space there. Or your agent can call the casting director to possibly get you another audition time. Be sure that the reason for changing the audition is important. If you have to, politely tell the casting assistant that you have an appointment; he or she may be able to get your child in a little sooner or at least let you know if they are running late.

Don't take the audition time if there will be a conflict. It looks bad for your agent and you if you show up and have to leave or if you don't show up at all. Chances are, if you do it once without a good explanation, your agent won't call again. If you have a cell phone, use it to call your agent if you have an emergency (such as car trouble) that will cause you to be late. That way your agent can call the casting studio and tell them.

It just may happen that your child will have more than one audition in a day. Count your lucky stars and hope they are running on time!

Allow yourself time to park, and consider the traffic conditions. If this is your first time at that studio, allow yourself extra time to find the place. Most casting studios have very little street parking and no lot parking, and you may have to walk a couple of blocks.

Place

Write down the place of the audition and the address. Auditions can be held in a number of places, from hotels to the casting agent's office. Many cities have specific casting studios, while television and movie auditions can be at the studios themselves. If this is the case, allow yourself a little more time to get there because it can take a while to walk through the lot and find the casting office.

Casting director

Keep a record of the person who is responsible for casting. You will get to know the casting directors in your area. When your child has seen one, it can put him or her at ease to know that they have seen that person before. You will eventually get to know the nuances of each director. Some you know will expect your child to be prepared, some will be more relaxed, and some will give you feedback. It can also be encouraging to go back to a director that has already booked your child before.

Knowing who the casting director is can also come in handy when you send a thank-you note.

Project

Always keep track of the name of the project your child is auditioning for. It is a quick way of recognizing the project that you are being called back for. For toy commercials, record the name of the product. For films or television, write down the name of the show and if it is a series, movie of the week, or feature film.

Scene

Knowing what scene your child will be auditioning for can help you choose what to dress him or her in. For example, if the commercial is for a new toy set at a playground, you wouldn't dress your son in a suit and tie. If your little girl will be doing somersaults, you may want to put on shorts underneath her dress. However, you may not always receive this information.

Consider taking an instant or digital photograph of your child just before the audition and staple it to your audition tracking form.

Lines mean that you are given the complete script and sides mean that you have only a portion of the script. They are commonly called the same thing.

If you don't have a fax machine at home, find one in your area that you can receive faxes. Some corner stores offer this service for a fee.

Appearance

Make a brief note of what your child wore to the audition. If your child gets the callback, he or she should look the same, and it can jog your memory if you have it written down. Sometimes you are given specific instructions for what to wear. The casting director may want your child to be a fairy princess or to wear a bathing suit. Most of the time, the dress for auditions is casual. You may want to note how you have done your child's hair (e.g., spiky, pulled back, new haircut).

A word of hard-won advice: Do not give your child a blue bubble gum ice cream cone, or red slurpee in the car on the way to the audition. Anything that will leave a messy color on you child's face will show up on camera.

Lines, sides, and storyboards

Your agent should know if lines or sides are needed for the audition. Sometimes, however, there will be sides at the audition that your agent doesn't know about. Circle the category on the form that applies. Of course, for small babies, there will be no lines. If there are only one or two lines, they may be given to you at the audition.

Once at the audition, you will usually be given a storyboard to review with your child. A storyboard is a cartoon drawing of what will happen in the commercial or scene. It is often an indication of what your child will do in the audition. (See Sample 10 for an example of a storyboard.)

Sides and storyboards can be available on the Internet if your agent is using an Internet breakdown service. Your agent can also fax them to you.

If you receive lines before an audition, make every effort to help your child be ready. Much of how successful your child is depends on how well you know and work with your child to learn the lines.

Get to know what works best for your child. Some children are very serious and approach learning lines in a serious manner. Others may work better if you make the lines a fun game. Age is an important consideration. Your ten-year-old son might like to work on his lines by himself until he thinks he knows them, then go over them with you. A preschooler will need help to learn lines.

STORYBOARD

Baby's
Best
Diapers®

Make sure your child knows his or her cue (i.e., when to say the line). Try not to tell your child how to say the line. For example, if your three-year-old daughter has to say, "Are you awake?", talk with her about the ways you could say the line: Loud, like you are waking her up, or quietly, like you aren't sure if she is awake yet. Then let her do it the way she is most comfortable. In the audition, the casting director may ask her to change the way it is said. If you have practised different ways and she is asked to change, it won't fluster her.

If you are given lines days before the audition, the casting director expects your child to be prepared. However, you should consider how reasonable the timeline is. Use common sense. If there is no way your child can learn all the dialogue before an audition, let your child learn what he or she can. It is better to have the child be comfortable with what has been learned, than to be overwhelmed or nervous about what hasn't been learned.

Casting directors may call in three or four children at a time to audition. The casting assistant might have these children line up in their group, or, if they are to be interacting with another child, they may be paired in specific groups. If there is an adult auditioning with your child, it may be a good idea to have your child say hello and review the scene with that adult. Remember that this adult is going in for the job too, and he or she wants the audition to go as well as it can.

Callback dates

Your agent may or may not know when the callback dates are, but this information should be available at the audition. You need to make a note of the callback date in order to keep your calendar organized and to avoid booking conflicts.

Note that in film and television, if your child is called to a pre-screen (i.e., a meeting with the casting director), there may be no audition and there won't be any callback dates.

Shoot dates

Your agent should know when the production will shoot. Again, you need this information to keep your calendar organized and to avoid booking conflicts.

Expenses

Jot down if you had to pay for parking, or if your son needed to be a cowboy and you had to buy a hat. As a rule you shouldn't have to spend any money on auditions. Talk to your agent to see what is expected.

If you are self-employed, you may be able to deduct these expenses. Check with your tax accountant.

Got callback

If your child gets the callback, underline the date in red and add the time. Using this form will help you keep organized. It will also help to evaluate how your child is doing. You can measure how often your child is getting callbacks, how many auditions your child is going on, and who is seeing your child. After the first six months, you may want to discuss the results with your agent.

I am often asked, "How many auditions should my child go on before he or she gets a part?" There is no answer to that question. Somewhere there is an average statistic that says a child has to go on 40 auditions before he or she gets a part. I have also seen many children get the part on the first audition they go on. That is what makes this business frustrating. You take your child to many auditions, you are about to quit, and then your child gets a part. As long as your child is enjoying going to auditions, hang in there.

When your child doesn't want to go to an audition, listen to him or her, and find out why. Take a break, and don't go on auditions for a while. Your child's reluctance will show up on camera and you may be wasting everyone's time — as well as making your child miserable.

Some guidelines for making auditions go smoothly

You have all your audition information, you know where you are going, and you have allowed yourself plenty of time to get there. Now what? Follow these guidelines for making auditions go smoothly and you and your child will have a better chance at enjoying the process — and at success.

Take only the child that is going to audition

If it is at all possible, please leave siblings, grandma, grandpa, aunts, uncles, and anybody else at home. Only one parent should take the child to an audition. If two parents have to go, one should wait elsewhere.

If a casting director is going to see 25 children in the course of an hour, and each one brings one parent, that is at least 50 people coming and going in the studio. The waiting area in casting studios is usually small. There just isn't room to accommodate hundreds of people if everybody brings unnecessary bodies. While waiting, the noise level has to be kept to a minimum, so the fewer people there, the better.

Check in with the assistant when you arrive

Check in with the assistant when you arrive at the studio, just like you would at a doctor's office. The assistant will give you a form to complete. The layout of the form can change but the information needed is consistent. As you become familiar with the different casting studios, you will know where the forms are and you can fill them out before you check in.

Use Worksheet 3 to record details about your child so that you always have this information handy. Remember to update height, weight, and clothes size regularly. These are some of the things the form will ask for:

☆ Child's name.

☆ Name of agency, agent, and telephone number.

☆ Child's height, weight, and clothes size, including shoe size.

☆ Can your child do a special activity that is needed in the commercial? This can range from turning cartwheels to roller-blading. Don't lie. It can embarrass you and your child if he or she is asked to do something he or she can't do.

☆ Do you have any conflict with the callback dates or the shooting dates?

Callbacks could be spread over a couple of days, so if you have a previous commitment on one of those days, indicate what day is good for you. Carefully consider what would prevent you from going to a callback. Shooting can also be spread out over a couple

A woman once brought her entire daycare because one child had an audition. The fewer people at an audition, the better.

Union auditions require a sign-in sheet that asks for the union number. If your child is not a union member or an apprentice member then leave it blank, but do fill in the rest of the form.

WORKSHEET 3
CHILD'S INFORMATION

For infants, fill out this sheet often. For older children fill out at least every three months.

Date: _____ Age: _____

Height: _____ Weight: _____

Waist: _____ Inseam (length from crotch to ankle): _____

Shirt size: _____ Pants/skirt: _____ Shoes: _____ Jacket: _____

Date: _____ Age: _____

Height: _____ Weight: _____

Waist: _____ Inseam (length from crotch to ankle): _____

Shirt size: _____ Pants/skirt: _____ Shoes: _____ Jacket: _____

Date: _____ Age: _____

Height: _____ Weight: _____

Waist: _____ Inseam (length from crotch to ankle): _____

Shirt size: _____ Pants/skirt: _____ Shoes: _____ Jacket: _____

Date: _____ Age: _____

Height: _____ Weight: _____

Waist: _____ Inseam (length from crotch to ankle): _____

Shirt size: _____ Pants/skirt: _____ Shoes: _____ Jacket: _____

Date: _____ Age: _____

Height: _____ Weight: _____

Waist: _____ Inseam (length from crotch to ankle): _____

Shirt size: _____ Pants/skirt: _____ Shoes: _____ Jacket: _____

Date: _____ Age: _____

Height: _____ Weight: _____

Waist: _____ Inseam (length from crotch to ankle): _____

Shirt size: _____ Pants/skirt: _____ Shoes: _____ Jacket: _____

of days. Toy advertising can shoot three or more commercials in a week. If there is an unavoidable conflict, write it down. If you have a family vacation to Disneyland planned that you are not prepared to cancel if your child gets a part, do not take the audition in the first place. Always keep your agent informed if you are going to be away.

Some commercials ask if you want your child to be background or an extra on the commercial. This is entirely up to you. It can be good experience for the child and something to add to his or her college fund. There is always the possibility that your child could be upgraded on the set. (See Chapter 6 for more information on being upgraded.)

After you have neatly filled out the form, return it to the casting assistant. Be ready with a headshot if it is asked for or the casting assistant may take a Polaroid shot of your child. Then you wait for your turn.

Keep yourself occupied

Waiting around at auditions can be a frustrating and boring experience, especially if it is not your first audition and the experience is no longer new. You need to find ways to keep both yourself and your child occupied while you wait.

I recommend that you keep an auditioning backpack at home. In it keep snacks, juice box, crayons, coloring books, and other quiet things that your child can use to stay amused. If your daughter has objections to someone else playing with her dolls, then don't bring them. There are usually lots of kids at auditions.

Try to keep your child relatively quiet. If you are lucky, you won't have to wait at all. You arrive, your child goes in, it takes only a few minutes, and you leave.

Auditioning is the only time you should be out of sight from your child.

Familiarize yourself with the proceedings

While you are waiting, review the storyboard if you haven't seen it before. If it is necessary, someone will tell the children any special instructions. Tell your child to listen for his or her name so he or she can answer when called. Point out the person who will take your child into the audition room.

For the first audition, explain to your child that he or she will be going into the audition room alone. When infants are being auditioned, sometimes a parent will take them in. As soon as the children are toddlers, they are asked to go into the audition by themselves. This is the only time that your child is out of your sight.

What if my child is reluctant to audition?

If your child doesn't want to go with the casting director or assistant, don't push, convince, threaten, or cajole. When a child is reluctant or timid, the casting director will usually just go on to the next one. With commercials costing hundreds of thousands of dollars to make, the producers simply cannot afford a child that seems reluctant to work. The casting assistant might offer to let your child go in later, but this is very unusual so don't expect it.

As a parent, try not to get discouraged. It may just be how your child was feeling that day, or your child didn't like the look of the person he or she was to go with. Once, I heard a boy say he had to go to the bathroom and that's why he didn't want to go in. Ask your child if he or she has to use the bathroom before you check in. Being reluctant twice in a row might make you consider holding off on auditioning for a while. Talk to your agent. In this case, maybe a class will help your child's confidence level. Perhaps you have to ask yourself if this is right for your child.

What happens in the audition?

The room your child goes into will have the casting director, a camera with a cameraperson, and perhaps some executives for the product.

Your child will be asked to go to the *mark*. A mark is a piece of tape on the floor. Then your child will be asked to *slate*. In younger children, this means stating their name and maybe their age. As they get older, slating is saying their name, and the agency they are with. Sometimes children are asked to do a *profile*, which is turning sideways, both sides, to the camera.

The casting directors are all very professional and are used to dealing with children. They will properly guide younger ones and most often tell them they did a great job. As the children get older, there is less personal attention and a polite thank-you is all the children get at the end.

When your child comes out of the camera room, don't interrupt the casting director to find out how your child did. Don't ask the casting assistant how your child did, or when they will call you. This is definitely a "don't call us, we will call you" business. Unless it is bad feedback (as in, I do not want to see that child again), you don't get any feedback from commercial auditions. Any feedback will come to your agent and he or she will pass it along to you.

What time will auditions be held?

Part of the commitment in the film and television industry is the time spent on auditioning. For school-aged children, the industry is trying to make audition times after school, but sometimes auditions during the morning can be unavoidable and you will have to pull your child from school. For toddlers and infants, auditions can be held at any time.

Some auditions are held in the evenings. There are guidelines in many states and provinces that regulate how late an audition time can be, especially on school nights.

You must have the means to get your child there. If you have to arrange for someone else to take your child, make sure he or she has this guide so they have the information for the forms.

Never say to your agent that you will be there and then leave the arrangements for the last minute. You put an agent's reputation, the very heart of his or her business, on the line if you don't show up for an audition.

6
WORKING BACKGROUND

Background performers are what used to be called extras. Many children will find a little taste of movie magic by working background. Some parents in the industry believe that background work is beneath their child, and that they should only do "star" or principal work. However, because many children will not ever get to do principal roles, background work can be a chance to be part of a movie.

Background work gives you and your child some idea of what it is like to be "on set." Doing background can be outright fun. Your child may be tobogganing on fake snow in the middle of July or playing with a really cool toy. However, he or she may also be sitting in a cold, wet tent, waiting for hours to be standing in a busy crowd doing nothing. It all depends on the project.

Work as a principal and working background are two very different things. Follow the advice in this chapter, and your child's time spent working background will be enjoyable and relaxing for both of you.

Scheduling your time

Whatever the project you're working on, there will be lots of waiting time. Always be prepared with activities. Bring along things you know your child enjoys doing. It will be a lot easier for both of you if you have things for your child to do during the wait. If your child is school age, bring along homework.

When you are booked for background, be sure that you are prepared to spend the whole day. Don't schedule other appointments or activities for that day. You may have only a four-hour call, but it can easily run over.

If you have committed to doing a certain number of days, be sure that you are available for all those days. If a scene is going to be shot over a few days, then the same people will have to be in the scene at all times. A booking that lasts for more than one day is called *continuity*. Continuity can be a number of days spread out over the length of the whole shoot. For example, if the film is set in a classroom, then continuity will have the same children in the classroom for all the scenes. You may be working in segments of two or three days over a period of weeks. If you sign up for this kind of project, be sure not to change your child's look during the length of the shoot — no haircuts, perms, or changing hair colors.

Working conditions

The number of people working on a project can influence the working conditions of background work. The area where background performers wait is called the *holding*. The facilities for holding 100 people may not be as comfortable as the facility for 10 people. The meal for 200 may be a little less appealing than eating off the catering truck when there are only a few people working. (But as usual, there is no consistency. Be prepared for anything. If you have worked on a series as a background performer you may know the conditions the second time you get called.)

Upgrading

Background work is unpredictable and you have to be prepared for anything.

One of the reasons many parents have their children work background is the possibility of an upgrade. This is where a person is given lines, thus upgrading his or her status to actor, or even principal. While this does happen, don't count on it.

Both the Screen Actors Guild (SAG) and the Alliance of Canadian Cinema, Television, and Radio Artists (ACTRA) have very specific regulations about what constitutes an upgrade. There is a common misunderstanding that if the director even talks to the child they are immediately upgraded to actor category. This is not so.

If your child is asked to do something on set other than what he or she was already doing or was contracted to do, call your agent and tell him or her what is happening. If your agent is unavailable, then write down what your child is doing. There may be contracts to sign later and it can be helpful if you know exactly what your child did.

Some tips for working background

The most important rule is no matter what your child is doing: **Be within sight and sound of your child at all times.** Never leave the set or let your child wander off alone. If you are taking your child to the bathroom or if craft services is some distance away, let the person in charge know where you are.

When your child is working, watch what he or she is doing. If there is a break in filming, it can be helpful if you can review what your child did or where he or she was before returning to the set. Although there are people who do direct your child, you knowing is also important.

Remember what scene your child is in. Although it is not your responsibility, the wrangler may ask what children have already been used or were used in a particular scene. Pay attention to what is happening.

Do not change your child's appearance after he or she has been seen by hair and makeup. If your daughter has long hair and you have to pin it back so she can eat, remember to let it loose before she returns to set.

Don't let your child go back to set carrying anything. Sometimes your child may be playing with a toy or eating a snack and will go back to the set with something in his or her hand. If your child is given a prop to use, give it back to the prop person on the way from the set or be sure you know where it is. If the prop is left with your child, then you are responsible for it.

If you are asked to sign a contract on set, don't be afraid to ask if production can fax a copy to your agent before you sign it.

Because there is no specific time for coffee breaks, the craft services table was developed. Food must be available for the cast and crew so they can have a snack when they need one.

Keeping track of the details

When your agent calls to book your child for background, use Worksheet 4 to help you keep track of all the information.

Location

Make sure you get all the directions when you are given the location address. The location may range from a studio shoot to a farmhouse way out in the country. If it is available, you should get a copy of a location map (see Sample 11). You may be asked to report to either background/extras holding or the assistant director at the circus.

Project and scene

Record the name of the film, commercial, or television show. You will usually be told what scene your child will be in. This information is useful so that you know how to dress your child. It will tell you if your child is playing in the snow or shopping at the mall.

Wardrobe

Unless it is a specific costume, or in some cases, continuity, background performers provide their own wardrobe. There are some basic rules for wardrobe. The most important is that there should be no logos, sayings, or decorations on your child's clothing. Brand endorsement is big business, and some movies have contracts with certain brand names to show the brand in the movie. If your child is wearing a logo of a competing brand, it can cause problems for the production company.

Bring at least three changes of clothes for the wardrobe people to see. You should be given suggestions of what to bring depending on the scene being shot. Mark your child's name and telephone number on the inside of the garment. That way, if it is left behind, there is a chance that the item may get returned to you.

Bring your child's wardrobe in a proper garment bag or gym bag. Don't just throw the clothes into a plastic bag where they can get soiled and wrinkled. Bring clothes that your child is comfortable in. Throw in an oversized shirt that your child can wear over his or her clothes to keep clean. If the weather is wet or cold, pack extra socks and a warm jacket. You are better off to overpack than to have a wet, cold, miserable child on your hands.

WORKSHEET 4
BACKGROUND TRACKING

BACKGROUND WORK
Day/date:
Time:
Location:
Project/scene:
Wardrobe:
Wrangler/AD:
Expenses:

BACKGROUND WORK
Day/date:
Time:
Location:
Project/scene:
Wardrobe:
Wrangler/AD:
Espenses:

BACKGROUND WORK
Day/date:
Time:
Location:
Project/scene:
Wardrobe:
Wrangler/AD:
Expenses:

BACKGROUND WORK
Day/date:
Time:
Location:
Project/scene:
Wardrobe:
Wrangler/AD:
Espenses:

SAMPLE 11
LOCATION MAP

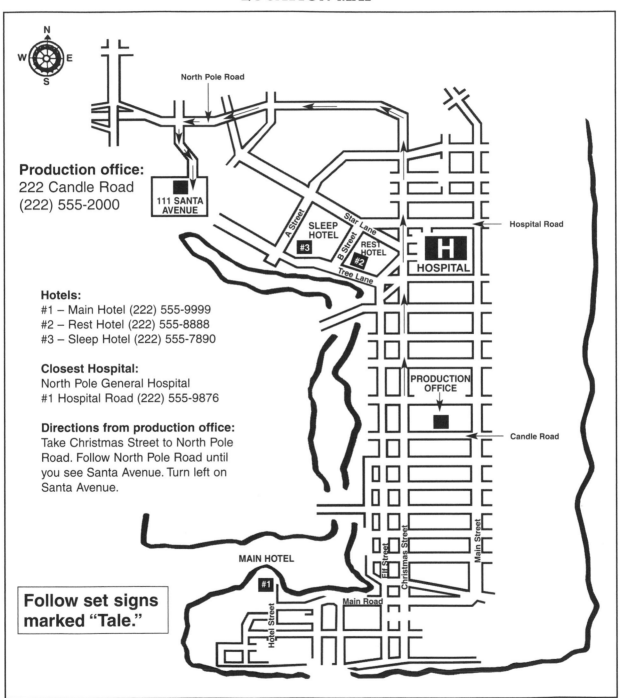

Production office:
222 Candle Road
(222) 555-2000

111 SANTA AVENUE

North Pole Road

A Street
B Street
Star Lane
Tree Lane

SLEEP HOTEL #3
REST HOTEL #2

H HOSPITAL

Hospital Road

Hotels:
#1 – Main Hotel (222) 555-9999
#2 – Rest Hotel (222) 555-8888
#3 – Sleep Hotel (222) 555-7890

Closest Hospital:
North Pole General Hospital
#1 Hospital Road (222) 555-9876

Directions from production office:
Take Christmas Street to North Pole
Road. Follow North Pole Road until
you see Santa Avenue. Turn left on
Santa Avenue.

PRODUCTION OFFICE

Candle Road

Main Street
Christmas Street
Elf Street

MAIN HOTEL

#1

Hotel Street

Main Road

Follow set signs marked "Tale."

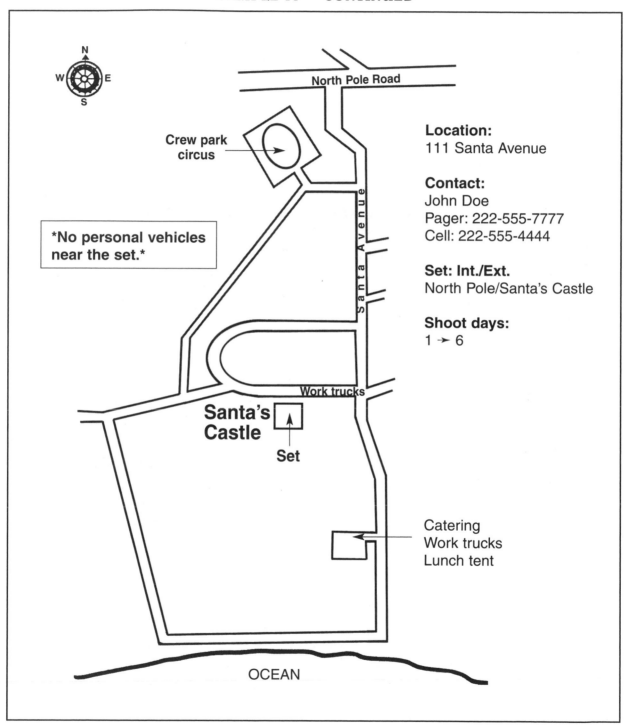

North Pole Road

Crew park circus

No personal vehicles near the set.

Santa Avenue

Location:
111 Santa Avenue

Contact:
John Doe
Pager: 222-555-7777
Cell: 222-555-4444

Set: Int./Ext.
North Pole/Santa's Castle

Shoot days:
1 → 6

Work trucks

Santa's Castle

Set

Catering
Work trucks
Lunch tent

OCEAN

There is also a code of dress that applies to parents. No pornographic logos or sayings of a sexual nature are permitted on set. This is written in the contracts for many production personal and should be respected by parents as well. Be sure to dress yourself warmly and comfortably. Remember that you too may be on your feet for the better part of the day.

Wrangler/assistant director

The wrangler or assistant director is the person that you would report to on set. A wrangler looks after the background performers. Sometimes, if there are a lot of children on set, the production company may hire a children's coordinator. Or you may have to report to an assistant director. Try to get a telephone number of a contact person on set in case you have an emergency on the way.

The wrangler will tell you when your child is needed. He or she is in touch with the set and knows what is happening. The wrangler knows what is being shot and may have some idea as to the working time frame. You have a right to know the time frame, but don't pester him or her with questions.

Expenses

Keep track of your expenses if you have to pay for parking or buy any special items. There shouldn't be any expenses with working background but keep track of anything you may have to buy.

Background performer vouchers

When your child works background, there will always be some kind of voucher or form for you to fill in. Read it carefully and try to print neatly and firmly as you can be making up to five copies. The form will usually ask for the following:

- ☆ UBCP/ACTRA **number.** This is the permanent membership number assigned to your child from his or her union. Your child may be a full member of the union or an apprentice member. **Note:** SAG does not have an apprentice program.

- ☆ **Performer's name**. This is your child's name, not yours.

- ☆ **Agent.** If you have gotten this engagement from sources other than your agent, then leave this area of the form blank. If you have gotten this engagement from your agent, you must check the box "Mail check to agent." Always have your agent's address and telephone number when you go to the set, and try to be complete when you are filling in this part of the form.

☆ **Social Security/Insurance Number.** If your child has a Social Security/Insurance Number, then fill in the blank.

☆ **Date of birth.**

☆ **Call time.** This is the time you were told to be on set. If you arrived early, as you should, put the proper call time in the space. The crew call will be given to you from the wrangler or the assistant director. Don't just assume that it is the same time as your call time.

☆ **Location.** Fill this in as you were given it. It could be a street number or a studio.

☆ **Travel time and mileage.** You will not have to fill this out very often. Travel time and travel mileage are usually established with union approval before you go to the set. They are used only if the location is quite far away from the urban center. If you live in a rural town, you are not paid mileage to work background.

☆ **Meal times, wardrobe changes, and use of car.** These are filled out by the wrangler or assistant director.

☆ **Wrap time.** This is filled out by the wrangler or assistant director *before* you initial the form.

☆ **Rate and category.** Make sure that these are checked and are accurate.

Sample 12 shows an example of a voucher you will need to fill out if your child is working background in a nonunion production. Sample 13 shows an example of a union background performer voucher.

> You should apply for a Social Security/Insurance Number when your child starts work in the film and television business.

SAMPLE 12
NONUNION EXTRA VOUCHER

NONUNION EXTRA VOUCHER

Performer's name:	Jane Smith
Agent (If applicable):	Molly Starr ☑ mail check to Agent
Address (If no agent)	
	737 Big Bucks Lane, Hollywood
Zip code: 90210	**Phone:** 222-555-1111
S.S.N.:	**If child, D.O.B.:** 15/05/99
Production name:	Child's Tale
Producer:	Bigshoes Ltd.

Date:	20 June 200-
Call time:	06:00 a.m.
Location:	Hill Street
1ST meal from 08:00 a.m.	**to** 08:30 a.m.
2ND meal from	**to**
Wrap time:	10:00 a.m.
Bike Reimbursement	
Vehicle Reimbursement	
Pet Reimbursement	
Misc. Reimbursement	

EXTRA CASTING: CD   **ASST. DIRECTOR:**   **APPROVED FOR PAYMENT:**

TYPE OF CALL: _____

RATE PER HOUR $ 10.00
(Includes vacation pay and agent's fee.)

BACKGROUND PERFORMERS NONUNION SHEET
AUTHORIZATION TO REPRODUCE PHYSICAL LIKENESS

"I agree to accept the sum properly computed, based upon the time and the basic rate shown, as payment in full for all services heretofore rendered by me for the company named above. I hereby give and grant to the company named above all rights of every kind and character whatsoever in all to all work heretofore done and characters whatsoever in and to all work heretofore done, and all poses, acts, plays and appearances heretofore made by me for you and in all of the results and proceeds of my services heretofore rendered for you, as well as in and to the right to use my name, likeness and photographs, either still or moving for commercial and advertising purposes. I agree that said company may use or refrain from using, all or any part of my photograph(s) and may alter or modify if in any configurations, technology and/or systems and in any manner or media now known or hereafter devised. I further give and grant to the said company the right to reproduce in any manner whatsoever any recordings heretofore made by the said company of my voice and all instrumental, musical or other sound effects produced by me. I further agree that in event of a retake of all or any of the scenes in which I participate, or of additional scenes as required (whether originally contemplated or not), I will return to work and render my services in such scenes at the same basic rate of compensation as that paid to me for the original taking. I release said company from any claims, demands, losses or other liabilities on any basis whatsoever arising out of its use of my name, likeness and/or photograph. I shall not assert any claims against said company arising out of such use. I understand that the results and proceeds of my rendition of services hereunder shall be deemed as work-for-hire for you in connection with a motion picture production and you shall be deemed the author thereof for copyright purposes. My sole and exclusive remedy for your breach of this release shall be an action for damages and I irrevocably waive any right to equitable or injunctive."

DECLARING YOUR RESIDENCY

1. For my services described above, I will render such services and will be paid as (Check One).
   EMPLOYEE ☐   SOLE SHARE ☐   MULTI SHARE ☐   OTHER ☑ Self _____

2. By virtue of birth, naturalization of landing, I am lawfully in the United States of America and I am and will at all material times be ordinarily resident (183 Days or more) in the USA for the purpose of income tax:
   YES ☑   NO ☐   (Check One).

3. Date of landing or naturalization:
   I was a resident of California on December 31st of the year preceding the one in which principal photography of the production commences:
   YES ☑   NO ☐   (Check One).

4. I file personal income tax returns as a resident of California and have done so or will do so for the income tax year immediately preceding the one in which principal photography for the production commences:
   YES ☑   NO ☐   (Check One).

5. I understand that the applicant will be relying on this declaration for the Federal and State labor tax credits which may be subject to government audit, and hereby warrant that the above-noted information is true and correct.

Signed by

X _Jane Smith_ _____
EMPLOYEE

June 20, 200-
DATE SIGNED

UNION BACKGROUND PERFORMER VOUCHER

BACKGROUND PERFORMER VOUCHER
Member and Permittee

PLEASE PRINT CLEARLY

MEMBER #: 000 NONMEMBER #:	DATE: 20 June 200-
PERFORMER'S NAME: Jane Smith	CALL TIME: 06:00 a.m.
AGENT (if applicable): Molly Starr ✓ Mail Check to Agent	LOCATION: Hill Street
ADDRESS: 737 Big Bucks Lane	TRAVEL TIME: ½ hour MILES: 30
Hollywood	____ NONDEDUCTIBLE MEAL AT (time):
ZIP CODE: 90210 TELEPHONE #: 222-555-1111	FIRST MEAL: 8:00 a.m. to 8:30 a.m. __ Penalty
SSN:	SECOND MEAL: to __ Penalty
IF CHILD, DATE OF BIRTH: 15 May/199-	WARDROBE CHANGES: 1 ✓ 2 __ 3 __ __
PRODUCTION NAME: Child's Tale EPISODE:	____ TRANSPORTATION:
PRODUCER: Bigshoes Ltd. TELEPHONE #:	WRAP TIME: 10:00 PERFORMER'S INITIALS: JS

RATE: ____ 4 HOUR CALL   ✓ 8 HOUR CALL

Joe Producer

PRODUCER'S SIGNATURE

Jane Smith

PERFORMER'S SIGNATURE

CATEGORY: (CHECK ALL CATEGORIES WORKED)

__ BACKGROUND PERFORMER	__ WARDROBE CALL
__ SPECIAL ABILITY	__ PHOTO-DOUBLE
__ STAND-IN __ PHOTO SESSION	__ OTHER: ____

SECOND CATEGORY: Start Time: End Time:

7
HOW TO BEHAVE ON THE SET

What looks like chaos on the set is actually a well-orchestrated production. All those people running around each has a job and knows what to do. How you and your child behave on set can determine whether things run smoothly for you. Your behaviour can also play a part in determining whether you are called back for future work with this production company. Some of the following tips seem basic, but you would be surprised at how badly some parents and children behave on set. Make sure you aren't one of them.

As a parent of a child working in the film or television industry, you must obey one golden rule: **Look after your child and his or her best interest.** (See Chapter 8, which outlines some of the basic working conditions for children in the industry.)

What to do on set

DO stay within sight and sound of your child while on set. Not only is it your right but in many places it is also the law. If the set is very crowded or small, you should be able to watch the filming from the video circus. Don't be intrusive about it. A production assistant will tell you where you should stay.

DO arrive at the location 15 to 30 minutes early. You will be given a call sheet (see Sample 14) that outlines where you should be and when.

DO have your child ready to work. If he or she has lines, make sure they are learned.

DO be sure your child is rested beforehand.

DO have all local permits, your child's Social Security Number and I-9 identification in the United States and Social Insurance Number in Canada. (See Chapter 8 for more information on working permits.)

DO check in with the designated person on set.

DO introduce yourself to the tutor or teacher, if it is necessary for one to be on set.

DO escort your child to the classroom area, but wait outside the classroom.

DO be polite and courteous to everyone on set.

DO supervise your child at the craft services and catering.

DO make sure that you appoint a responsible chaperone if you are not going to be on set with your child. Be sure the chaperone knows how to behave on set.

DO speak up if you feel your child needs a break or is being asked to do something he or she should not be doing.

DO let your agent know if your child has any special food or medical requirements before you go to the set.

DO sign out at the end of the day.

DO go with your child to hair and makeup, or anywhere else on set.

DO help your child get into wardrobe, if needed.

DO stay out of the way. Sets are busy places with people and equipment moving all the time.

DO tell the person you reported to if you and your child are going to be away from the circus or holding area.

DO shut off alarm watches and put pagers and cell phones on vibrate and silent. A sure way to look like an idiot is to have your cell phone start ringing during filming.

DO bring along a folding chair for yourself and an activity for you to do.

SAMPLE 14
CALL SHEET

CALL SHEET DAY #1 of 89
Monday, June 17, 200-

NO FORCED CALLS, OVERTIME, OR TURNAROUND WITHOUT PRIOR APPROVAL OF PM OR CO-PRODUCER

Starr Entertainment, Ltd.
Tel: 222-555-9990
Director: John Doe
Producers: John Doe, Jane Doe
Executive Producer: Jolene Doe
Writers: Jack Doe, Janine Doe
Co-producer: Justine Doe

Sunrise: 6:19 a.m.
Sunset: 9:20 p.m.
Weather: Sun and cloud
P.O.P.: 40% HI: 18 LOW: 10

Nearest hospital: Alaska General, 1 Hospital Road
Set phone: 222-555-6767

CREW CALL: 7:00 a.m. (on set)
Shoot call: 8:00 a.m.
Location: Northpole, 111 Santa Avenue

SCENE #	SET/DESCRIPTION	CAST	D/N	PGS	LOC
21	INT SANTA'S CASTLE — FOYER	2, 3, 4, 5, 6, 15	Day 1	3-1/8	1
	Elf greets Santa's return, introduces Rudolph	A			
		Total pages:		3-1/8	

CAST		CHARACTER	P/U	MU/H/WDRB	REHEARSE	ON SET	LOC	REMARKS
1.	John Doe	Santa	Travel LA to NP		- -			TBA
2.	Jane Doe	Mrs. Santa	5:45 a.m.	6:15 a.m.	- -	8:00 a.m.	1	Pick up at hotel to set
3.	John Doe	Elf	5:45 a.m.	6:00 a.m.	- -	8:00 a.m.	1	Pick up at hotel to set
4.	John Doe	Elf	5:45 a.m.	6:30 a.m.	- -	8:00 a.m.	1	Pick up at hotel to set
5.	Jane Doe	Rudolph	6:30 a.m.	7:00 a.m.	- -	8:00 a.m.	1	Pick up at hotel to set
6.	Jane Doe	Child	HOLD IN ALASKA					
15.	Jane Doe	Child	HOLD IN ALASKA					

ATMOSPHERE

A.	10 Children		6:30 a.m.	7:00 a.m.		8:00 a.m.	1	Pick up at hotel to set

STUNTS

A.	Stunt Coordinator John Doe	on own			7:00 a.m.	1	

STAND INS:

Santa	John Pope	on own			7:00 a.m.	1	
Rudolph	Jane Pope	on own			7:00 a.m.	1	

SPECIAL NOTES

CREW NOTE: There will be a courtesy shuttle leaving from the hotels for those who want a lift.
PROPS: Santa's Bag, Sleigh
GRIP: Phoenix Crane with Tech
VISUAL EFFECTS: Snow
TRANSPORT: 1 tonne to move sleigh

#	ON SET	CALL	#	ON SET	CALL	#	ON SET	CALL
Production			**Costumes**			**Miscellaneous**		
Director	John Doe	7:00 a.m.	Costume designer	Jane Doe	7:00 a.m.	Unit publicist	John Doe	7:00 a.m.
UPM	John Doe	7:00 a.m.	Asst costume designer	Jane Doe	7:00 a.m.	Extras casting	John Doe	7:00 a.m.
PM	John Doe	7:00 a.m.	Cost. Dept. Coor	Jane Doe	7:00 a.m.	Tutor	John Doe	7:00 a.m.
1st AD	John Doe	7:00 a.m.	Key costumer	Jane Doe	7:00 a.m.	Dialect coach	John Doe	7:00 a.m.
2nd AD	John Doe	7:00 a.m.	Set supervisor	Jane Doe	7:00 a.m.	Aerial coord	John Doe	7:00 a.m.
2nd 2nd AD	John Doe	7:00 a.m.	Asst set supervisor	Jane Doe	7:00 a.m.	**Medic/Craft service**		
3rd AD	John Doe	7:00 a.m.	Truck costumer	Jane Doe	7:00 a.m.	First aid/craft	John Doe	7:00 a.m.
TAD	John Doe	7:00 a.m.	BG costumer	Jane Doe	7:00 a.m.	Asst first aid	John Doe	7:00 a.m.
Daily PA	John Doe	7:00 a.m.	Daily costumes	Jane Doe	7:00 a.m.	**Caterer**	**Onset catering**	
Continuity	John Doe	7:00 a.m.	**Make-up and hair**			200 breakfast hot and ready from		7:00 a.m.
Camera			Key MU	Jane Doe	7:00 a.m.	200 crew lunches @ 12:30 p.m.		1:00 p.m.
DOP	John Doe	7:00 a.m.	Asst MU	Jane Doe	7:00 a.m.	**Production**		
Steadicam/Bcam	John Doe	7:00 a.m.	HB MU	Jane Doe	7:00 a.m.	Associate producer	John Doe	on call
A 1st AC	John Doe	7:00 a.m.	Daily MU	Jane Doe	7:00 a.m.	Prod executive	John Doe	on call
A 2nd AC	John Doe	7:00 a.m.	Key hair	Jane Doe	7:00 a.m.	Prod coord	John Doe	on call
B 1st AC	John Doe	7:00 a.m.	Key hair	Jane Doe	7:00 a.m.	Travel coord	John Doe	on call
B 2nd AC	John Doe	7:00 a.m.	Key hair	Jane Doe	7:00 a.m.	2nd asst prod coord	John Doe	on call
Loader	John Doe	7:00 a.m.	**Art department**			Super prod acct	John Doe	on call
Trainee	John Doe	7:00 a.m.	Prod. Designer	Jane Doe	7:00 a.m.	Asst to director	John Doe	on call
Stills	John Doe	7:00 a.m.	Super art director	Jane Doe	7:00 a.m.	Asst to director	John Doe	on call
Video			Art director	Jane Doe	7:00 a.m.	**Visual effects**		
Video Pback Coord	John Doe	7:00 a.m.	Art dept. coord	Jane Doe	7:00 a.m.	Vis effects super	Jane Doe	on call
Grip			Const coord	Jane Doe	7:00 a.m.	Vis effects prod	Jane Doe	on call
Key grip	John Doe	7:00 a.m.	Head painter	Jane Doe	7:00 a.m.	Vis effects wrangler	Jane Doe	on call
Best boy grip	John Doe	7:00 a.m.	Set decorator	Jane Doe	7:00 a.m.	Vis FX coord	Jane Doe	on call
A dolly grip	John Doe	7:00 a.m.	Asst set dec	Jane Doe	7:00 a.m.	Motion control op	Jane Doe	on call
B dolly grip	John Doe	7:00 a.m.	Greensperson	Jane Doe	7:00 a.m.	Motion control asst	Jane Doe	on call
Grip (w)	John Doe	7:00 a.m.	Best boy greens	Jane Doe	7:00 a.m.	VFX asst	Jane Doe	on call
Daily grip	John Doe	7:00 a.m.	On set carpenter	Jane Doe	7:00 a.m.	**Locations**		
Key rigging grip	John Doe	7:00 a.m.	On set painter	Jane Doe	7:00 a.m.	Loc manager	Jane Doe	on call
BB rigging grip	John Doe	7:00 a.m.	On set dresser	Jane Doe	7:00 a.m.	Asst. loc. mgr	Jane Doe	on call
Electrical			**Property**			TAL	Jane Doe	on call
Chief lighting tech	John Doe	7:00 a.m.	Prop master	Jane Doe	7:00 a.m.	Loc PA	Jane Doe	on call
Gaffer	John Doe	7:00 a.m.	Asst props	Jane Doe	7:00 a.m.	Security	Jane Doe	on call
Best boy	John Doe	7:00 a.m.	Asst props	Jane Doe	7:00 a.m.	**Transportation**		
2nd best boy	John Doe	7:00 a.m.	**Special effects**			Trans coord	Jane Doe	on call
Board operator	John Doe	7:00 a.m.	Coordinator	Jane Doe	7:00 a.m.	Trans captain	Jane Doe	on call
Electric (w)	John Doe	7:00 a.m.	1st assistant	Jane Doe	7:00 a.m.	Picture car capt	Jane Doe	on call
Genny op	John Doe	7:00 a.m.	SFX	Jane Doe	7:00 a.m.	Driver	Jane Doe	on call
Rigging gaffer	John Doe	7:00 a.m.	SFX asst	Jane Doe	7:00 a.m.	Driver	Jane Doe	on call
Sound			SFX supervisor	Jane Doe	7:00 a.m.	Driver	Jane Doe	on call
Sound mixer	John Doe	7:00 a.m.	**Stunts**			Motorhomes (9)		
Boom operator	John Doe	7:00 a.m.	Coordinator	Jane Doe	7:00 a.m.	Honeywagon (1)	Sound van (1)	
Cable person	John Doe	7:00 a.m.	Stunt rigger	Jane Doe	7:00 a.m.	Make-up trailer (1)	Wardrobe trailer (2)	
						24-pass busses (3)	Camera trucks (2)	
						Minivans (3)	Washroom trailer (1)	
						Grip trucks (2)	SFX truck (1)	
						Electric rig truck (1)	VFX truck (2)	
						Electric truck (2)	Gym trailer (1)	
						Props truck (2)	Craft service cubes (2)	
						Cable truck (1)		

DO bring activities for your child to do.

DO keep your ears open. There is usually someone with a walkie-talkie nearby and you can hear what is generally happening on set.

DO fill in all paperwork clearly and legibly.

DO ask the production assistant if you can get a copy of the call sheet if you have not been given one previously.

What not to do on set

DON'T ever leave your child unattended on set.

DON'T bring any other person but the working child to the set — not both parents, not siblings, not relatives, not neighbors, not anyone else.

DON'T interrupt your child while he or she is being tutored.

DON'T leave the set while your child is being tutored.

DON'T let anyone convince you to let your child do anything that you feel is unsafe or not in your child's best interest.

DON'T make demands to the producers, directors, or assistants about having more camera time, upgrades, or using your child more.

DON'T sit in a chair if it doesn't have your name on it.

DON'T interrupt anyone. If you see people that have moved away from the set, chances are they are having a private conversation. Someone standing by themselves may be on the telephone using an earpiece. Be aware and don't just barge in to chat.

DON'T pack your bags and pockets with snacks from craft services.

DON'T invite anyone who is not involved in the production to join you for lunch.

DON'T take your camera to the set to get pictures of the stars working. If you want to take a picture of your child working, ask the wrangler or production assistant. He or she might be able to arrange for you to get permission.

DON'T complain about waiting, especially if you are working background.

DON'T take resumes and photos of friends and relatives to the set to show them around and try to get them work.

"Watch your back" is the expression that tells you someone is moving equipment and to look out.

DON'T take Girl Guide cookies, cleaning supply catalogues, or raffle tickets to the set in order to try to make some sales.

DON'T let your child share a dressing room with an adult or with a child of the opposite sex.

DON'T change your child's appearance after he or she has been through wardrobe, hair, and makeup.

DON'T back out of your commitment. If you are booked to work for a certain number of days or time, be sure to honor your commitment.

DON'T be the parent that everybody talks about negatively. Your reputation as a stage parent can influence your child's career. No one has a problem with you looking out for your child, but you must remember that your child is part of a team.

DO have fun!

8
WORKING CONDITIONS FOR CHILDREN

Whether your child is working as a background performer or is the lead in a feature film, you should always know the conditions he or she is working under. Many states and provinces have specific conditions for employment of children in the film and television industry. Unfortunately, many do not.

As a parent, you must be familiar with the laws in your area. Your agent should be able to cover them with you or, at the very least, tell you where to get a copy of any regulations set out by the local government. A great source for these laws is your local ACTRA, SAG, or AFTRA office.

If you live in an area that has no laws in place, use the conditions outlined in this chapter as guidelines for your child's working environment.

Most of the filming in the United States is done under SAG or AFTRA contracts. Some states recognize the Codified Basic Agreement with SAG and AFTRA, which covers conditions for minors

The basic condition governing your child's working condition should be common sense.

working in film. Any production working under the SAG agreement will abide by SAG rules and regulations, no matter where the production location is. This is referred to as SAG Global Rule One. The information in this chapter is an amalgamation of the laws for most of North America. Use these conditions as guidelines for your child's working condition.

Parent must be present

This is the number one golden rule: The parent must be on set within sight and sound of the child and is responsible for the child at all times while the child is on set. The child shall not be in a one-on-one situation with an adult other than the tutor or teacher without the parent being present.

The key word here is responsible. Regardless, of what country, what contract, or what union your child is working under, your responsibility is to your child. The parent is the ultimate authority.

Never let a production company assign a guardian to your child. No one can replace a parent, but it can happen that you cannot be with your child on set. If you need to, be sure that you assign someone you trust will look after the interest of your child. A child's guardian is as fully responsible as you are on the set. A parent may assign a chaperone proxy to a child over two. This is not a guardian and this person has no legal authority over the child to provide consent on behalf of the child. A chaperone is only a temporary babysitter for your child if you cannot be on set.

Performance requirements

Child not required to perform in dangerous situations

No child shall be required to work in a situation that places the child in clear and present danger to life or limb or if the child or parent believes the child is in such a situation. If you feel your child is in danger, speak out. The situation will be reviewed and discussed with the parent and child. If the child persists in his or her belief, regardless of its validity, the child shall not be required to perform in such situations.

Physical, athletic, or acrobatic activity

When the child is asked to perform physical, athletic, or acrobatic activity of an extraordinary nature, the child's parent must be advised of the activity before the engagement of the child. If the child is fully capable of performing such activity, the parent must expressly inform the employer's representative of this fact.

Parent's written consent required for all stunts

A stunt is the performance of dangerous risks not normally expected of the average performer. The employer must secure the written consent of the parent before any child may perform a stunt. The parent may refuse to allow the child to perform the stunt.

Work with animals

A child shall not be required to work with an animal that a reasonable person would regard as dangerous in the circumstances, unless an animal handler or trainer qualified by training and/or experience is present and the handler or trainer can guarantee the safety of the child.

Children employed in scenes depicting child abuse or carnal acts

When a child is employed to perform in a scene that depicts child abuse, nudity, or carnal acts, the employer must consult with the parent and make available to the child and his or her parent a qualified mental health professional (e.g., psychiatrist, psychologist, social worker) to assist the child in preparing before participating in any such depiction. A child shall not be present during such scenes unless it is essential for the child to be on-camera.

Some states and provinces have their own laws. For example, there is a law under the labor standards act that is independent of any union jurisdiction in British Columbia that states: A child shall never be unclothed on set or anywhere he or she may be seen by anybody other than the parent.

Responsibility of the parent

Parent actions are subject to review

The parent must be familiar with the above regulations. This is a pretty vague condition. Some areas issue permits on a yearly basis. This condition was written to cover cases in which a child is doing something dangerous or working in poor conditions. If the parent says he or she didn't know, he or she may have his or her child's working permit revoked.

Parent must accompany child when traveling

The parent must accompany the child when traveling to a location in which the child will be housed overnight. The employer shall be responsible for all travel, food, and accommodation expenses.

Parent must be familiar with child's role

The parent must review the child's script or discuss any role the child is employed to portray with the employer before the child commences employment.

Permits

As a parent, it is your responsibility to get the necessary permits to allow your child to work. Make sure you do this well in advance — you don't want missing permits to hold up production. Each state and province has different permit requirements. Speak to your agent or local union office for more information.

School permit

The parent shall ensure that the school has been notified before the child starts employment and that the necessary school permit has been obtained. Some permits are issued through school departments and some through labor departments. School permits may be different from work permits and may be required separately.

Working permit

It is the parent's responsibility to obtain a working permit, often before work can start. Some permits are issued on a yearly basis, some are issued on a per job basis. Work permits are usually obtained through Labor Standards Offices, school superintendents' offices, or your local union offices.

Checklist 3 includes information that may be required for a work permit.

CHECKLIST 3
PERMIT APPLICATION

The child's parent or legal guardian must obtain a working permit for a child to be employed as a performer in the film, television, and radio and television commercial industries. The following checklist includes some of the information that the work permit application requires:

Child's Information

- ❏ Date of application
- ❏ Permit number, if it is a renewal
- ❏ Full legal name
- ❏ Complete address
- ❏ Home phone number and/or an alternate phone number
- ❏ Birth date
- ❏ Talent agent's name, address, and phone number

Parent or Guardian Declaration

- ❏ You must declare that you are legally responsible for the child.
- ❏ You must read and comply with the Employment Standards Conditions for the employment of children in the film, television, and television and radio commercial industries.
- ❏ You must agree that you or a chaperone, 19 years of age or older, will supervise the child at all times while on set.
- ❏ You must declare responsibility for the child's well-being and safety while the child is on the set.
- ❏ You must ensure that the child maintains the requirements of his or her educational program.
- ❏ You must include your name, address, phone number, and signature.

The child's employment permit application will also need to be endorsed by the child's school authority. A principal, teacher, or counselor employed at the school at which the child is enrolled may complete the form.

Note: A home-schooled child must have the school or agency at which he or she is enrolled with fill out the permit application and provide a copy of proof of enrollment.

The following is some of the information required by the permit application:

❑ Confirmation that the child named is a student enrolled at the school or agency named in this part of the application

❑ The current grade level of the child

❑ Name of the School District or District number

❑ The complete address of the school or agency

Principal, Teacher, or Counselor Declaration

❑ The authority must have met with you to discuss how the child's employment will affect the child's education and conduct.

❑ The authority must understand that he or she can contact the Employment Standards Branch if there are any concerns regarding the child's continued employment.

❑ The authority must sign his or her name and state his or her position with the school or agency. The authority must also include a contact phone number.

If the permit is granted, the Director of Employment Standards may order a review after the child has worked 20 days. If a review is ordered, the Director of Employment Standards will check with the school or agency authority to make sure the child is maintaining the requirements of his or her educational program.

Note: Employment Standards for children may differ from state to state or province to province. Please see your local labor standards office, school superintendent, or local union for information regarding child employment.

Canadian Union Work Permit

In Canada, in order to work on a union production, film, television, or commercial, if you are not a member of ACTRA, then you need to get a permit to work on that production. Your agent will take care of the paperwork, but the costs of the permits will be deducted from your income. The cost per permit depends on the category.

Emergency medical authorization

The parent shall sign an Emergency Medical Authorization Form, which shall enable the employer to obtain emergency medical treatment (if necessary) for the child.

Parent disclosure

The parent shall disclose to the employer, in writing, any medical history or condition or any attitudinal or psychological condition of his or her child of which the parent is aware that might foreseebly interfere with, or have an impact on, the child's ability to carry out the role for which the child is being considered.

Working hours

Rest and recreation

The parent will work closely with the employer to ensure that adequate rest and recreation is provided for the health and safety of the child.

Five-out-of-seven-day work week

The parent shall not allow the child to work more than five out of each seven consecutive day period. Permission may be granted for a sixth day of work by the proper authorities (e.g., the department of labor or other government department that issues the working permits). A seventh consecutive day of work is prohibited.

Hours of work for children

I cannot stress enough how important this subject is in your child's working career. It can be the most abused condition of employment. Production companies have been known to choose locations

Shooting can cost thousands of dollars a minute and production companies will try to push the limits in order to save money. Laws have been put in place for a very good reason. Don't be intimidated into letting your child be overworked. You also have a responsibility to be reasonable.

where there are no work-hour laws in effect. You are the ultimate authority over your child, and you must look out for him or her. If you see your child needs a break, tell the assistant director.

Some states and provinces will issue special permission to work outside the standard hours under special circumstances. Special circumstances may include location availability, early-morning or late-night exteriors, or live television productions.

In the United States, according to the SAG contract, the following are the hours at the workplace (including meal and tutoring times):

☆ Under 6 years — 6 hours

☆ 6 to 8 years — 8 hours

☆ 9 to 15 years — 9 hours

☆ 16 to 17 years — 10 hours

Note: SAG general contract meals must be served within six hours of call time.

In Canada, the following are the hours at the workplace (including meal and tutoring times):

☆ 15 days to 2 years — 8 hours. For each 15 consecutive minutes before camera, there must be a minimum 20-minute break.

☆ 3 to 5 years — 8 hours. For each 30 consecutive minutes before camera, there must be a minimum 15-minute break.

☆ 6 to 11 years — 8 hours. For each 45 consecutive minutes before camera, there must be a minimum 10-minute break.

☆ 12 to 14 years — 10 hours. For each 60 consecutive minutes before camera, there must be a minimum 10-minute break.

The work day cannot start before 5 a.m. and may not go later than 10 p.m. on a school day, regardless of whether a child is receiving tutoring on set. The child can work no later than 12:30 a.m. on an evening before a nonschool day, unless it is in the summer months when the child is not attending school. The child cannot work later than 2:00 a.m. A child cannot have fewer than 12 hours between call times.

Meal break

A child may not work more than five consecutive hours without a minimum half-hour meal break. The employer shall provide healthy snacks.

Working with infants

Infant defined

An infant is a child less than 2 years old and more than 15 days old. A child less than 15 days old will not be allowed to work.

Minor defined

According to the ACTRA contract, a minor is a child younger than the age of 17. For minors older than the age of 14, provisions for ages 12 to 14 should apply.

SAG defines a minor for —

☆ commercials, 15 and younger;

☆ film, television, or industrial work, 18 and younger;

☆ Network Code REF, 15 and younger;

☆ public radio, radio programming, and radio commercials, "school-age"; and

☆ public television, younger than 15.

Physician's statement

It is recommended that the parent get a written statement from a physician confirming that the infant is in good health and if there is any reason why the child should not be employed. If the employer requests such a statement, they are responsible for costs incurred to obtain it.

Adequate facilities for infants

The employer will provide adequate sanitary facilities for the care and rest of infants when employed. This will include a crib, change table, and a quiet and warm area where the infant may be fed and may rest without being held.

Exposure to light

An infant shall not be exposed to light greater than a 100-foot candle intensity for more than 30 seconds.

Handling infants

Hands should be washed before and after handling infants, and before and after diaper changes. Infant accessories must not be exchanged from one infant to another without first having been sanitized.

Altering an infant's appearance

When substances are used for altering an infant's appearance, provisions should be made for bathing the infant. Foods that commonly cause allergic reactions should not be used to alter the appearance of the infant's skin unless a medical doctor specifically approves their use. These foods may include, but are not limited to, raspberry and strawberry jams, jellies, preserves, and peanut oil.

Schooling

The glamor of having your child in the movie business cannot overrule your responsibility for your child's schooling. Schooling while working is mandatory. Usually the tutoring on set is more intense than classroom school, especially if yours is the only child on set. Some children produce better quality work with three hours of one-on-one tutoring than a month at regular school. Take advantage of this extra education and look at it as one of the perks of the business. Be diligent about keeping on track with the required tutoring time.

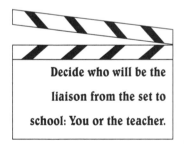

Decide who will be the liaison from the set to school: You or the teacher.

If your child is on a long shoot, assign one person from his or her school to keep in touch with. It could be a homeroom teacher, the principal, guidance counselor, or other school official. Give this person's name to the production office and the on-set teacher. That way, any schooling questions can be handled by the same person, thus avoiding confusion.

If you are filming a long way from home, have communications set up with your child's school for getting assignments. Keep your child's learning abreast of his or her class. If the home school's teacher requires the submission of assignments, arrange for mailing or delivery.

A laptop computer can be a great tool for your child. Be sure to tell the production staff so that they can arrange for a proper power source and possibly a telephone outlet for e-mail.

Try to give the child's school ample time to prepare schoolwork for the child to take to the set. If it is at all possible, have the on-set teacher talk directly with someone from your child's school to discuss what work is to be done during shooting. Any exams or quizzes should be administered.

If your child is older or in high school, the teacher and tutor should work together to make allowances for labs and other special classes. If your child is involved in drama, video productions, or media arts there may be a special opportunity for your child to get extra credits or learn something special behind the scenes. Talk with the tutor, the assistant director, and the school about making the most of the situation.

Commercial shoots are usually one or two days, so on-set tutoring is not required. Under some union agreements, two days is the maximum a child can work without tutoring; in some agreements it is three. All teachers/tutors must be qualified in the state or province where they are to tutor. If a child is from another country, the tutor may be a teacher qualified from that country's jurisdiction, provided that the teacher has submitted to a Criminal Records Reviews Act search and no relevant criminal record exists. In California, a teacher must have two credentials, elementary and secondary. The SAG agreement states that children from California must bring a teacher with them when working out of state or country.

The employer is responsible for providing an adequate teaching area that is quiet, clean, heated, and adequately lit. They are also responsible for basic class supplies and appropriate furniture. Do not accept a moving bus or car as an adequate schoolroom.

Tutoring time should not be less than three hours in a day. If your child is on set for an extended time, tutoring should not take place on more than five days of the week. Banking tutoring time by putting in a few hours on a Saturday or an extra hour on other days may be an option. Banked time must be used within 30 days of banking the time and by the end of the production schedule. Keep accurate records of the time your child is receiving tutoring. The employer also must keep records. Homework is not considered tutoring time.

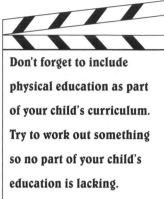

Don't forget to include physical education as part of your child's curriculum. Try to work out something so no part of your child's education is lacking.

The tutor/teacher may have to provide a parent or school with a weekly report as to the progress of the child.

Where a child's regular instruction is primarily in a language other than English, the producers shall use their best effort to provide instruction in that language.

Wages for time on set

All children shall be guaranteed a minimum of four hours' pay, including time that may be less than four hours. Tutoring/teaching time is considered work for purposes of payment of wages.

Dressing/change rooms

No child shall be required to share a dressing room or change in a room with an adult or a minor of the opposite sex.

Child's coordinator

When there are six or more children, in some areas less, one individual shall be assigned to all matters relating to the welfare and comfort of the children. The employer shall notify the parents of the children with the name of the coordinator. The comfort and welfare of the children shall be the only responsibility of the coordinator.

It is highly recommended that the employer require that the coordinator has undergone a Criminal Records Search and have no criminal record.

9

THE UNIONS, THE MONEY, AND WHAT YOU REALLY WANT TO KNOW

Working in a union

There is a distinct line in the film and television industry between two types of work — union and nonunion. The need for unions was born in the days when an actor was solely "owned" by the film studios. Since 1936, the Screen Actors Guild (SAG) has been establishing working conditions and payment scales for the film and television industry.

In 1943, Canada started its own union, the Alliance of Canadian Cinema, Television, and Radio Arts (ACTRA). Both unions have very similar contracts and working conditions, but the major variance is in the payments. SAG has a payout system for residuals that are paid out when a project runs. ACTRA has a system that pays at the time of doing the work based on a formula, and not when the project runs. (See later in this chapter for more information on residuals.)

Actors' unions have specific agreements that apply to commercial, television, or feature work. Each agreement can be hundreds of pages long with thousands of clauses. When your child books a union job, contact your local office of the appropriate union and get a copy of the agreement that applies to the project your child will be working on. Take the time to read the agreement and make yourself familiar with the conditions, especially those that refer to the actual working environment for children.

Many film and television projects are done outside union jurisdictions. Commercials are often filmed without union signatory agreements; they are the largest nonunion employers of children. Independent films and student films are often nonunion shoots. Sometimes you can get union permission to work on student films if you are a member of a union.

One of the advantages of working union is that you receive union scale payment. If the shoot is a nonunion, then the pay can be anything. Some states have legislation that requires payment not be less than minimum wage after the agent takes commission.

A union shoot is also protected with maximum hours of work and specific meal times. If you work a nonunion shoot, you will not be protected by a governing body to oversee hours or conditions, unless the conditions are covered by state or provincial laws.

All unions collect fees, dues, and benefit deductions. In Canada, if your child is not a member of ACTRA, then you must pay a permit fee to the union that will allow the child to work on the project. When a child becomes a union member, or apprentice member, that permit fee is no longer required.

ACTRA has an apprentice structure. After obtaining one permit for union work, a child may join ACTRA as an apprentice member.

Sample 15 shows an example of a commercial engagement contract that you will have to sign when you work on a union production. (Each union will have a similar contract.)

Payment scales and minimum rates

Payment scales and payment categories are specifically defined for all unions involved in the entertainment industry. If the project is nonunion, there are often no restrictions on how little the payment may be. Some areas have laws that set minimum wages, but be aware that in some states and provinces, film and television are exempt from local laws.

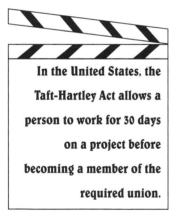

In the United States, the Taft-Hartley Act allows a person to work for 30 days on a project before becoming a member of the required union.

COMMERCIAL ENGAGEMENT CONTRACT

THIS PART TO BE COMPLETED PRIOR TO PRODUCTION

CONTRACT #: _____ BRANCH CODE

AGENCY (NAME OF ENGAGER) Commercials Ltd. (AGENCY PRODUCER) Joe Producer

ADDRESS 780 Big Bucks St., Hollywood 90210

SPONSOR Dollmaker

PRODUCT Doll

PRODUCTION HOUSE Bigshoes Ltd.   CHECK IF PAYING SESSION FEE ☐

ADDRESS 222 Famous Ave., Hollywood (PERFORMING COMPANY WHERE APPLICABLE)

TO SUPPLY THE SERVICES OF Jane Smith (PERFORMER'S NAME)

(PERFORMER'S ADDRESS) INCLUDE CITY / ZIP CODE 111 Actor St, Hollywood 90210   (TELEPHONE #) 222-555-1111

SOCIAL SECURITY # 000 000 000

FULL MEMBER NUMBER 0000   IN THE PERFORMANCE CATEGORY

APPRENTICE OR NONMEMBER WORK PERMIT NUMBER

DATE	TRAVEL TIME FROM HOME	TRAVEL TIME TO LOCATION	CALL TIME	MEAL TIME FROM	MEAL TIME TO	FINISH TIME	TRAVEL TIME FROM LOCATION	TRAVEL TIME TO HOME	DATE	CALL TIME	FINISH TIME
06/20/200-			10:00 am	1:10 pm	1:40 pm	4:30 pm			06/17/200-	WARDROBE CALL ✓	1 hr.
										AUDITION CALL ☐	
										HOLDING CALL ☐	
										SUBSTANTIAL SNACK YES ☐ NO ☐	

PERFORMER'S PLEASE INITIAL IN THE BOX   AGREE JS   DISAGREE   WITH THIS CONTRACT INDICATE WHICHEVER APPLICABLE   ENGAGER'S REPRESENTATIVE'S INITIALS _____

WORK REPORT: IT IS IMPORTANT THAT THE FOLLOWING REPORT BE COMPLETED AT THE END OF PRODUCTION AND FORWARDED TO THE ASSOCIATION WITHIN 48 HOURS TO ENSURE PROPER PAYMENT. MEMBERS CAN BE FINED FOR FAILURE TO FILE THIS REPORT.

PLEASE NOTE THAT PAYMENT FOR THIS WORK SESSION MUST BE RECEIVED IN THE ASSOCIATIONS OFFICE NOT LATER THAN 15 WORKING DAYS AFTER COMPLETION OF THE WORK SESSION IN ORDER TO AVOID LATE PAYMENT PENALTIES. SESSION AND RESIDUAL FORMS SUPPLIED BY THE ASSOCIATION UPON REQUEST MUST BE USED WHEN SUBMITTING PAYMENTS.

NUMBER OF NATIONAL COMMERCIALS   TV ☐ RADIO ☐

DEMO COMM.	TV RADIO	PRESENTATION DEMO	TV RADIO	TAGS	TV RADIO	SEASONAL COMM.	TV RADIO	REGIONAL CHANGES	TV RADIO

1

PUBLIC SERVICE ANNOUNCEMENT   TV RADIO   LOCAL & REGIONAL ADDENDUM   CAT. NO. TV RADIO   LOCAL & REGIONAL SHORT LIFE   CAT. NO. TV RADIO   DEALER COMM.   TV RADIO

SHORT LIFE ADDENDUM   TV   7 DAYS   14 DAYS   31 DAYS   45 DAYS   CHANGES   RADIO   7 DAYS   14 DAYS   31 DAYS   45 DAYS   CHANGES

INFOMERCIAL   TV ___ RADIO ___   ** If commercial is used on Internet, actor will be paid $1000.00.   DOUBLE SHOOT   JOINT PROMOTION   ** OTHER ___

SAG-ARTICLE 2404A (USA $) ___   X   SAG-ARTICLE 2404B (CDN $) ___

COMMERCIAL NAME OR NUMBERS   Doll 1   DOCKET NUMBER

(INSERT DETAILS OF FEES ABOVE MINIMUM WHERE APPLICABLE: OR "MINIMUM FEES")

SESSION Minimum   RESIDUAL Minimum   OTHER Minimum

PERFORMER'S SIGNATURE Jane Smith   DATE June 20, 200-

PRODUCER'S SIGNATURE Joe Producer   DATE June 20, 200-

SIGNATURE FOR PERFORMING COMPANY   DATE

PERFORMER'S AGENT

CHILD UNDER 16

DATE OF BIRTH

PLEASE PRINT CLEARLY

Your child may book his or her very first audition and get an eye-popping check within weeks of signing with an agency. However, it is more than likely that you will be taking your child to audition after audition before he or she will get a part.

Table 1 outlines the approximate minimum daily fees for different categories of performers. This table is based on the Union of British Columbia Performers' scales, but is within the range for rates across North America.

Background rates

If you have signed your child with a background agent, a background assignment may come first. Background work is the lowest payment scale on the union's pay requirements.

Daily minimum rates apply to an eight-hour day. Overtime kicks in after that. If it took less than eight hours to do your part, you still get paid the eight hours. The only time you will receive less than eight hours pay is if you are brought in to work background for a four-hour call. You do not receive less than those scales.

Additional fees are paid when you provide special clothing, you change your clothing more than three times in one day, and rough or dangerous work is involved. Productions must also pay extra if your child is not fed within a certain time frame — this is referred to as a *meal penalty*. Higher paying categories include stand-in, photo double, and special ability background performer.

Actor rates

The minimum daily fee for a day performer according to SAG is $636.00. The minimum daily fee for ACTRA's lowest category of actor (a person with six or fewer speaking lines), is $344.25.

These are the lowest fees for feature film and television. They do not include overtime or account for deductions. There are higher paying categories for both SAG and ACTRA in actor categories. There are also specific payments for appearances on television series and made-for-television movies.

Session fees and residuals

Commercial session fees range from a background performer at $340.00 to $557.00 for a principal performer. Commercials have a

TABLE 1
APPROXIMATE PAYMENT SCALES

MIMINUM DAILY FEES					
Category	Daily Fee (8 hours)	Hourly Rate	Overtime Rate @ 1.5x (8-11 hours/day)	Overtime Rate @ 2x (after 11 hours/day)	Weekly Rate (For a 40-hour, 5-day workweek)
Principal Actor/ Stunt Performer	$525.00	$65.00	$100.00	$130.00	$2,100.00
Variety Principal	$790.00	$100.00	$150.00	$200.00	$3,150.00
Actor	$355.00	$45.00	$66.00	$90.00	$1,400.00
Stunt Actor	$785.00	$100.00	$150.00	$195.00	N/A
Stunt Coordinator	$685.00	$85.00	$130.00	$170.00	N/A
Choreographer	$525.00	$66.00	$100.00	$132.00	$2,100.00
Chorus Performer	$510.00	$65.00	$95.00	$130.00	$2,050.00
Group Singers/Dancers	$395.00	$50.00	$75.00	$100.00	$1,575.00
Vocal/Dialogue Coach	$790.00	$100.00	$150.00	$200.00	$3,150.00

MINIMUM DAILY FEES FOR BACKGROUND PERFORMERS					
Category	Daily Fee (8 hours)	Hourly Rate	Overtime Rate @ 1.5x (8-11 hours/day)	Overtime Rate @ 2x (after 11 hours/day)	Weekly Rate (For a 40-hour, 5-day workweek)
Stand-in	$160.00	$20.00	$30.00	$40.00	$720.00
Photographic Double	$150.00	$20.00	$30.00	$40.00	N/A
General Background Performer	$150.00	$20.00	$30.00	$40.00	N/A
Specialty Ability Background Performer	$200.00	25.00	$40.00	$50.00	N/A

silent on camera (SOC) category that does not apply to film. This category pays the same as a principal.

These fees are for session work only. That is what your child would get paid for doing the whole day's work. Sample 16 shows what a payroll extra voucher looks like.

Residual payments are the fees paid to a performer every time the project is shown (e.g., every time a commercial is shown on television or a film screens in a theater). Residual payments are in addition to the hourly or session fees for shooting.

A session fee is the day's pay outside of any residual or other payments.

Residuals are based on how many market units are being used. Market units are based on the population of an area. For example, a commercial that is running in New York has a higher market unit value than a commercial running in Bolder. A commercial that is going to be run around the world will pay more than a commercial that is running only in New York. Both ACTRA and SAG have tables of market values and payment schedules in their agreements.

A commercial can pay as little as $100 if it runs in a limited market for a short time. If a commercial runs nationally for a long time, it could result in hundreds of thousands of dollars in residuals.

Residuals are separated from the session fee because the session fee is guaranteed income: Your child did the work and will get the pay. If on final editing the production does not use your child in the commercial, you will still receive the session fee, but will not receive residuals. Residuals are paid only to those children that are in the final commercial.

Canadian and US unions have different ways of paying residuals. Some Canadian residuals are paid before a commercial runs, based on the number of units that the advertiser already knows are going to run. In the United States, a production may hire a company to track when commercials are being aired and will process payments based on these units.

The residual system applies only to union commercials and film work. If your child is doing nonunion work, the money can be quite different. The session fees are somewhat lower, ranging from $300 to $700 a day. Instead of residuals, a lump-sum payout called a *buyout* is paid. The buyout fee covers a period of time, usually two or three years. The buyout does not rely on markets, or how often a commercial is running, or where it is running.

PAYROLL EXTRA VOUCHER

PAYROLL VOUCHER

PAYROLL DEPARTMENT

EXTRA VOUCHER

Date: June 20, 200-   Project: Child's Tale   Union #: 0000   Union: ☑ Yes ☐ No

Surname: Smith   First name: Jane   Initial: L.   Age: 9

Address: 111 Actor Street   City: Hollywood   State: CA   Zip: 90210

Phone number: 222-555-1111   Check box if —

☐ new employee
☐ new address

Check box if —
☑ child
☐ single
☐ married

Social Security #: 000-00-0000   (Social Security Number is mandatory for payment.)

TIME	RATE	SPECIAL COSTS	OTHER
Time in: 11:30 am	Basic rate: 25/hr.	Wardrobe: Qty ___ $ ___	Hair: $ ___
Time out: 4:30 pm	Rate Adj.:	Meal Penalty: Qty 1 $ ___	Beard: $ ___
Total hours: 5 hrs.	1.5x ___ : ___	Vehicle: $ ___	Special ability: $ ___
1st meal break	2x ___ : ___	Miles: 24	Smoke work: $ ___
Time in: 01:30 pm	Total: ___	Cent/miles: ___	Wet work: $ ___
Time out: 02:00 pm			Fitting: $ ___
2nd meal break		Total: ___	Uniform: $ ___
Time in: ___			Body make-up: $ ___
Time out: ___			Interview: $ ___
			Other: $ ___
			Total: $ ___

Approved by: JS

#000000

PLEASE READ CONDITIONS OF EMPLOYMENT:

By signing this voucher, I acknowledge that I understand the following conditions of employment and that I agree to each and every condition:

(1) That I have reviewed the information entered on this voucher and that it accurately represents my complete work information on the Production for the date indicated. I understand that this work information will be used to calculate my wages for this particular date and I agree that such wages computed will be payment in full for all services rendered by me;

(2) That I hereby grant to the Production Company of The Production, its successors, assigns, licensees, or other person or company who might gain title or rights to the Production the right to photograph me and record my voice to use, alter, dub, and/or otherwise change such photographs and recordings in any manner whatsoever and for any reason in connection with the The Production, such right to be world-wide and in perpetuity;

(3) That I represent that I am not now nor have ever been an employee of Payroll Management Company, Inc. or any other company connected with or operating under it as a dba, and further acknowledge that this voucher does not create an employment contract between myself and Payroll Management Company, Inc. or its subsidiaries;

(4) That as a condition of my employment by the Production Company on The Production, I further agree that I will abide by all rules of employment as dictated by the Production Company, or its agents, or by any Safety Coordinators assigned to The Production, especially those rules pertaining to safety including but not limited to: (a) remaining in areas designated as safe areas during any period that I am not asked to perform my duties as an extra; (b) acting in a safe manner at all times so as not to injure myself or others; and (c) to refrain from taking any illegal substances that might impair my ability to do the job for which I was hired;

(5) That as a further condition of employment herein, I agree that I have the ability to perform each and every task, job assignment, or special ability I have been asked to perform and that if I knowingly make false representations that I am qualified to perform these assignments when, in fact, I know that I am not qualified, that such misrepresentation may be grounds for dismissal of any workers' compensation claim should I be injured as a result of performing an assignment for which I knowingly was not qualified to perform; and

(6) In conclusion, I have read the entire conditions of employment and by signing this voucher, I acknowledge that I understand and agree with the entire conditions of employment.

Jane Smith

Signature

Under the SAG agreement, film and television residuals work much the same way as commercials. They are tracked and paid out to the performer as they are run. However, residuals work differently under the ACTRA agreement. A percentage of the session fee is added on at the time the session fee is paid and the performer receives no further payments until the payout period is over — usually four years. Then an amount equal to the first payout is paid.

Note: These are the minimum payments. Your agents can negotiate a better payment, or may sign a deal that will give you a percentage of the profit from the movie and other things such as guarantees to work in the sequel or production credits.

How long before I get paid?

Some states and provinces have strict time constraints for the handling of payments. Generally production should forward session payment to the union office within 15 days of shooting. It may take several weeks for the union office to process it. Then your agent has up to 30 days to send the payment on to you.

A residual payment should be submitted to the union office within 30 days of the first airing. There is no enforcing body to make sure your agent is paid in a timely fashion if the work is nonunion. A buyout check can come months after shooting a commercial.

Nonunion productions send payment directly to your agent. Once your agent gets the check, he or she then takes the deductions and passes along the remainder to you. In some states and provinces there are time limits that the agent has to get the monies owed to you after they are received from the production company. This is usually the time it takes for the check he or she received from the production company to clear the bank.

Your agent's commissions and deductions

When your child books a job, you should discuss the rate and other payment details with your agent before you go on set. You may be asked to sign a contract on set, and you want to know what you are signing. It is good practice to call your agent from the set

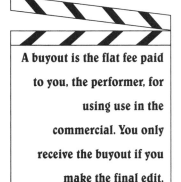

A buyout is the flat fee paid to you, the performer, for using use in the commercial. You only receive the buyout if you make the final edit.

before you sign anything, and you should make every effort to have the contract you are asked to sign faxed to your agent before signing.

When you get your check from the agent, look it over carefully, and understand what all the deductions are for.

Your agent will take a commission off the gross earnings before other production company deductions have been taken. In theory, an agent should only take commission from the actual session fees, hours worked, or residual payments. Your child can receive monies for other time involved with the project, but most agents do not take commission from this money. Other monies could include wardrobe fees, callback checks, expense checks, or per diem money.

In addition to their commission, some agents will deduct office costs and any mailing or shipping charges, and then mail you the remainder. Always be aware of what your agent is going to deduct from your child's check and what your agent can legally charge you for. Look at it carefully and do not be afraid to get explanations. Ask your agent to send a copy of the check he or she receives from the production company. See Chapter 2 for more information on what monies your agent can deduct.

Protecting your child's income

Unions and some states and provinces have taken steps to protect a child's income. In Canada, if your child has done more than $5,000 of work under union jurisdiction, then 25 percent of that income is put into trust until the child reaches 18.

In the United States, under the Coogan Law, 15 percent of all monies earned by a minor is withheld in a trust on behalf of the minor. Many states have also passed legislation that protects all of a child's income as his or her own property, not the property of a parent.

The Coogan Law has been revised in recent years. The law now applies to all minors' contracts, and in California, the income becomes the property of the child; not the communal property of the parents. For more information on the Coogan Law, call (323) 549-6639.

> Payroll companies will often include per diem money already paid to the performer on a paycheck. The same per diem is then deducted on the check from the production company; that way the production company has a record that they have paid you.

Even though there are laws to protect your child's income, you have a responsibility to see that the proper deductions are taken. Although many parents believe that they will always be saving their child's income, it is often difficult to do so when you are struggling to make the mortgage payments and your six-month-old gets a $3,000 check.

Protect your child's income and see that the proper trusts are set up from the beginning. It is also your responsibility to be sure the proper taxes are filed and any taxes are paid. Don't expect your agent to advise you on business matters, although most of them can tell you who can.

10
WHO DOES WHAT IN THE FILM AND TELEVISION INDUSTRY

When you read the credits of a film or television project, do you know what everybody does? The more your child becomes involved in the industry, the more people behind the camera you will get to know. As you learn how difficult the work is and how much work these people have to do, you'll get a greater respect for all the people involved in the film.

Each position within the industry is clearly defined by the unions or guilds representing them. When you are on set, one way to identify a person is to look at his or her walkie-talkie, which is usually on the belt. The person's department or position is usually marked on the walkie-talkie.

The brief descriptions of industry positions in this chapter are meant to inform readers and in no way intend to minimize the amount of work all these jobs take. For every job description I describe there are a hundred parts of the job that I haven't mentioned.

Note: The term "key" usually refers to the head of the department. These people are not only responsible for the things you see them do on set, but also have to prepare and report budgets, and do scheduling and purchasing.

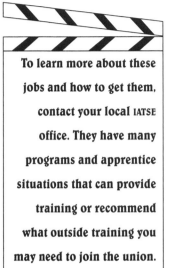

IATSE jobs

A huge number of jobs fall under the International Alliance of Theatrical Stage Employees, Moving Picture Technicians, Artists and Allied Crafts of the United States, its Territories and Canada, AFL — CIO, CLC, known as IATSE. This union is international and has branches in both Canada and the United States.

Director

The director works closely with all the members of the team, but in the end is the person responsible for the project. The director chooses locations, and participates in casting, rehearsals, and art department work. Of course, he or she directs the actors, camera angles, lighting, and a million other components of the project.

The director's work often starts years before the first camera ever starts rolling. In the hierarchy of the entertainment business the director, along with the producer, is "The Boss."

Second unit director

The second unit director directs scenes that usually contain no dialogue or he or she may direct the action sequences. He or she can be filming at the same time as the first unit is working, but at a different location. Second unit directors are responsible to the director and producer.

First assistant director

Called the first AD, the first assistant director is always on set. What you and your child will see this person doing on set is such a small part of the job. You will see a person communicating between the actors and the director, placing background people, working with the stand-ins, and making sure everything runs smoothly. What you don't see is the way the first AD has to organize everything, from preproduction to shooting schedules, to locations, to working with the heads of all the other departments.

This job is not only creative but also demands great organizational skills. An AD may have many assistants, as many as the size of the project requires. First AD is a specialized job, and good first ADs are in high demand.

> To learn more about these jobs and how to get them, contact your local IATSE office. They have many programs and apprentice situations that can provide training or recommend what outside training you may need to join the union.

> Unlike what its name implies, a first assistant director is not necessarily a stepping-stone into the director's chair.

Second assistant director

The second assistant director is usually the person that will tell you your call time. He or she does much of the communication between actors and background performers, and the production office. The second AD is usually the person on set with the call sheets. He or she may also be the person you check in with when you arrive on set. The second AD does a lot of paperwork and fills out a lot of reports.

Production manager, unit production manager, production coordinator, and their assistants

The production management team works to be sure that the logistics, budget schedules, locations offices, and personnel are set up and function properly. They are the people who run the offices, make sure that all the people are hired and the locations have been secured, arrange for the transportation and housing of crew, cast, and staff, and see to the day-to-day running of the project.

Accountants

Production accountants do as their job title describes, and like the tax accountant and the business accountant, their knowledge is specific to the entertainment industry. They do the all-important payroll.

Locations manager and assistants

The locations manager works closely with the director and producer to choose and make arrangements for location shooting. He or she has to negotiate property rental and use rates and obtain the necessary permission or permits for locations sites. The location manager works with assistants to secure police or security, and to arrange for cleaning of the location during and after the productions.

Production designer/art director

When a production is large and requires a person to coordinate art design, wardrobe, makeup and hair, set design, lighting and special effects, and accounting for all these departments, a production designer is hired. An art director does the same thing. The art department prepares sketches of what the project is going to

On set you will hear someone called a TAD. This is the trainee assistant director. This is the entry-level position of the assistant director program.

To register your house as a possible location, contact the film commission in your area.

look like. They set the artistic look of the picture, and design costumes, sets, lighting, set decoration, and any special effects.

Editing

Every production has editors for the picture, sound, music, and dialogue. If you are working on set and are in a position to see the raw film that has been shot (called the *dailies*), you will appreciate the work that an editor has to do. Films are very rarely shot in sequence. The middle may be shot first, followed by scenes from all different time frames. The film editors have to be sure that the picture flows smoothly, and the sound editors make sure the sound is right.

Sound team

Sound has changed a lot since the days when there was a piano player in the theater. It has become a very technical field. There can be many people on the sound team, often well into the post-filming stage. On set, the sound recorder will have his or her own station with a monitor tied into the recording equipment. While this might seem like a good place from which to watch the filming, be careful around this area. The technician needs the area to be clear because the equipment is sensitive, and like everything else on set, expensive.

Foley artist

The term foley artist originated from the early person who did the job. A foley artist is the person that manufactures sounds that match the action. For example, he or she may record walking on Styrofoam to make the sound of people walking in the snow.

Photography department

The director of photography sets the shot according to the director. One of the many skills he or she has to have is the ability to see a shot as it would be on the big screen — approximately 30 feet high — where every shadow and image is exaggerated. It is like creating 172,800 photographs that, when shown at the rate of 24 per second, create a motion picture. (I am lucky if I don't cut a head off at the top of my family photos!)

Working with the director of photography are the camerapeople, loaders, and technicians. Many types of cameras are used today to create effects like slow motion and high-speed action. Motion-capture cameras film images that are used to create computer images. Motion-control cameras use computers to control the movement of the cameras and require special skills to operate.

Gaffer

Gaffer is a simple name given to a tough job. The gaffer is the head technician of the lighting department. When you are on set you will see the gaffer directing the lights and moving screens and equipment — all for results you might not notice, but that are very noticeable to the director and director of photography. A gaffer's first assistant is the best boy. Other titles in the lighting department are rigging gaffer, wireman, lighting technician, and generator operator.

Grips

Again, this is a little name for a big job. Grips are responsible for getting and moving all the "stuff" on sets. This includes all the equipment needed for the production, such as sets, catwalks, platforms, dollies, cranes, or any other mobile camera or sound equipment. The key grip is the person responsible for all the work of the grips, dolly operators, and others in the department.

Greenspeople

It's an exciting thing to see a greens team transform a bare studio into a dense bush, or take a dense bush and make it safe for the actors to run around in. They also have to maintain the continuity of the trees, brush, and surrounding area throughout the shoot.

Makeup and hair artists

The makeup artist team ranges from special effect makeup to the people that check over the background performers. The hair and makeup people often share the same trailer. When on set, you will accompany your child to see both artists.

The clapper is a small board that holds information identifying a shot. Written on it is the working title, director, director of photography, the scene number and take, the date, and time. When it is clapped, that synchronizes the film and sound.

The person who does the clapper, or slate, works with the cameraperson and is also responsible for loading the camera with film.

If an actor needs contact lenses for the production, a licensed eye specialist is required for application and maintenance.

Construction/painters

Construction people and painters work together but are separate categories for the credits and union definitions. Some movie sets are huge construction projects that have been built to create what the director, producer, and writer have envisioned.

Property master/props

Every time you see an actor pick up a book or any other object, the prop department has been at work. They have to maintain the continuity of the props, buy them, and keep them in good order. When your child is on set and is working with props, be sure to return them to the propsperson when you leave the set.

Publicist

The publicity team is responsible for putting what information the director and producers want before the public. You may meet the publicist when they are having still shots done on set, or if this team is doing a "making of" the picture. You, not your child, may have to sign a release for this department to use your image when they are taking random shots for the film.

Script supervisor

The script supervisor is either within arm's length of the director or at the video circus furiously taking notes. Never interrupt a script supervisor when he or she is taking notes. He or she has to record a ton of information about the shot, including timing, if the actor says any word different than the script, details of action, positions, camera angles, slate numbers and prints, and continuity notes. At the end of the day, the script supervisor has to put all this into reports for the production office.

Set decorating

The set decorating team, under the set decorator's direction, consists of buyers, on-set decorators, dressers (who actually put the items on the set), drapers/upholsters, and assistants. They have to shop for the furnishings, like every other team, deal with budgets, put up and take down the set furnishings.

Colorist, color consultant

A film colorist makes sure that the color of the film is consistent, for example, that a blue shirt worn is the same blue in all the scenes. Consistent color depends on the type and brand of film, the camera used, and the developing techniques.

Special effects

For every minute of a special effect you see on film, there can be days of planning and filming that go into making that shot. Even something that looks as easy as moving a cobweb from the doorway can take time to set up, make (they don't keep spiders handy), and film. A special effects team can be a company that is hired by the production to do all the special effects on a project. The teams can be a large number of people depending on the effect and the size of the budget.

Video special effects

Video special effects are the special effects that are added into the film at the postproduction stage. Much of the video effects today are outstanding because of the use of computers. Sometimes, actual software has to be developed to produce the effect the director wants.

Matt artists

The best way to explain what a matt artist does is to give this example. In the movie *Star Wars: A New Hope*, Obi-wan Kenobi walks around a generator over what looks like a deep electrical pit. What he is actually walking on is a glass floor with the scenery painted on. It is one of the most convincing illusions in the business.

Teamsters

Under the umbrella of the teamsters union are not only all the drivers of the trucks and cars, but also the catering truck operators, the cooks, and their assistants. Animal trainers and wranglers as well as stunt drivers and boat operators are also included in the teamsters' union.

Producers

The title of producer has changed since the early days of film-making, but the basic function has not. The basic job of the producer is to see that the project gets made. The producer used to be the person responsible for the financing of the project. Now the production title has many variances.

Producer

Films, commercials, and television shows are never made without the producer. The producer is responsible for everything. He or she get the story or screenplay or whatever medium the project is based on (also called the "property"). Getting the property includes obtaining the rights to produce it.

The producer hires the personnel to work on the project, including the director. He or she works out the distribution deals and does the budgeting.

How directly the producers are involved in some aspects of the project depends on the individual. Some producers will be involved in casting; some will leave it up to the director and casting people. Some will be on set during the whole shoot, and some will be there only when necessary. You may meet the producer at the audition, or never see him or her during the entire shoot.

Executive producer

An executive producer can mean a number of things. On a film where the producer is not very experienced, the financial backers may request that a producer with more experience act as a watchdog over the newer producer.

Sometimes a person wants to contribute financially to a project but not be involved in the day-to-day working of the project. He or she will be an executive producer.

If an established name, a star, or known director attaches his or her name to a project, thus insuring that the project will be made, he or she is often given the title of executive producer.

Co-producers

A co-producer is one of a team of people that shares the responsibilities of all aspects of the production.

Associate producer

An associate producer is one that does not have final say in the project but has some responsibilities during production or has invested some amount of money in the project. An associate producer may also be a person that has done some of the development of the project, but hands the project itself over to someone else.

Line producer

Line producers are the people that work the day-to-day productions, usually with the producers. Their job is not exactly production manager, and not exactly producer, but somewhere in between. Many productions do not have line producers.

APPENDIX: ONLINE RESOURCES

The Internet is a wonderful resource for further information. The Web sites of the different associations, guilds, and societies often have excellent links to other areas of information. Most of the information is free (except for the Casting Workbook as mentioned in Chapter 2).

Academy of Canadian Cinema and Television
www.academy.ca

Academy of Motion Picture Arts and Sciences
www.oscars.org

Academy of Motion Picture Sound
www.amps.net

Alliance of Canadian Cinema, Television, and Radio Artists (ACTRA)
www.actra.ca

American Federation of Television and Radio Artists (AFTRA)
www.aftra.org

American Society of Cinematographers
www.theasc.com

A Minor Consideration
www.minorcon.org

Association of Talent Agents (ATA)
www.agentassociation.com

Canadian Society of Cinematographers
www.csc.ca

Canadian Actors' Equity Association
www.caea.com

Canadian Actors Resource
www.canadianactor.com

Casting Society of America
www.castingsociety.com

Casting Workbook
www.castingworkbook.com

Cinema Audio Society
www.ideabuzz.com/cas/

Classification and Ratings Administration
www.filmratings.com

Directors Guild of America
www.dga.org

Directors Guild-Producer Training Plan
www.dgptp.org

International Alliance of Theatrical Stage Employees (IATSE) and
Moving Picture Machine Operators
www.iatse.com

Internet Movie Data Base
www.imdb.com

Motion Picture Association
www.mpaa.org

Motion Picture Editors Guild
www.editorsguild.com

National Association of Talent Representatives (NATR)
www.agentassociation.com

Producers Guild of America
www.producersguild.org

Screen Actors Guild (SAG)
www.sag.org

Society of CameraOperators
www.soc.org

Society of Motion Picture and Television Engineers
www.smpte.org

Steadicam Operators Association
www.steadicam-ops.com

Union of British Columbia Performers (UBCP)
www.ubcp.com

Writers Guild of America
www.wga.org

GLOSSARY

You'll always remember the feeling you get when your agent calls to book your child's first job. Cheering, jumping up and down, and a lot of hugging usually accompany the call. Now is a good time to say thank you. Thank your agent. If you want, send a short thank-you note to the casting director.

Your agent will give you the time and location of the shoot. It will help a lot if you are familiar with some of the terms of the industry. On the set, it can seem like people are speaking a different language. Being familiar with the terms and abbreviations will make it a little easier to follow what is going on.

Abby Singer: The shot before the last shot of the day. Named in honor of former first assistant director, Abby Singer, who used to call the last shot of the day one shot too early.

Action: The command from the director for the scene to begin. It indicates that the camera is rolling.

ACTRA: Alliance of Canadian Cinema, Television, and Radio Artists

AD: Assistant director

Ad lib: Spontaneous dialogue without relying on a prepared script.

ADR: Automated Dialogue Replacement. Dialogue added to a scene in postproduction. Sometimes erroneously called "looping."

AEA: Actors' Equity Association; often called simply "Equity." This union represents stage actors and managers.

AFI: American Film Institute

AFTRA: American Federation of Television and Radio Artists. Represents radio artists and news broadcasters, and, in earlier times, television performers. In more recent times, however, television performers may be represented by either AFTRA or SAG, depending on the producer's contract. Discussions about merging the two organizations have been ongoing for several decades; recent television, film, and commercial contracts have been jointly negotiated.

AGMA: American Guild of Musical Artists

AGVA: American Guild of Variety Artists

Art director: Person who conceives and designs the sets.

ATA: Association of Talent Agents (in the United States)

Audition: A tryout for a film, television, or stage role. Usually auditions involve reading from the script, but they can also require improvisation.

Avail: A courtesy situation extended by a performer or agent to a producer indicating availability to work a certain job. Avails have no legal or contractual status. Also called *Holds* or *First Refusal*.

Background: Used to be called extras. On the set, "Background!" is a verbal cue for the extras to start their action.

Background casting director: The person responsible for hiring the background performers. Sometimes works with directors in placing background people in the shot.

Back to one!: The verbal cue for performers to return to the mark where they started the scene.

Beauty shot: On television soap operas, the shot over which the credits are rolled.

Best boy: The assistant to the chief electrician, or head gaffer.

Billing: The order of the names in the title of opening credits of a film or television show.

Bio: Short for biography.

Blocking: Setting the movements of the performers for the scene.

Booking: A firm commitment to a performer to do a specific job.

Boom: An overhead microphone, usually on an extended pole. The boom operator is the member of the sound department responsible for holding the boom pole, with microphone attached, over and sometimes under the actors. He or she is also usually responsible for placing radio microphones on actors.

Blue screen: Shooting in a studio against a large blue or greenish backdrop, which allows a background to be superimposed later on the final image. The actors must imagine the set they are on and be aware of the limitations of their movements.

Breakaway: Specially designed prop or set piece that looks solid but shatters easily. Breakaway props are often glass items.

Breakdown: A detailed listing and description of roles available for casting in a production.

Callback: A follow-up interview or audition.

Call sheet: A sheet containing the cast and crew call times for a specific day's shooting. Scene numbers, the expected day's total pages, locations, and production needs are also included.

Call time: The time an actor is due on the set.

Camera crew: With the director of photography as its chief, this team consists of the camera operator, the first assistant camera operator (focus puller), the second assistant camera operator (film loader and clapstick clapper), and the dolly grip.

Camera operator: The member of the camera crew who looks through the lens during a take. He or she is responsible for panning and tilting and keeping the action within the frame.

Camera wrap: When an actor is finished shooting for the whole production.

Casting director (CD): The producer's representative responsible for choosing performers for consideration by the producer or director.

Cattle call: A casting call that results in many people showing up.

Caterer: The person responsible for breakfast, lunch, and dinner on a set. (Different from craft services.)

CD-ROM: A compact disk that holds text, music, and images.

Changes: Clothing worn while performing.

Cheat: The actor's adjustment of body position away from what might be "natural" in order to accommodate the camera; can also mean looking in a different place from where the other actor actually is.

Checking the gate!: A verbal command to check the lens on the camera; if the lens is OK, the cast and crew will move on to the next scene or shot.

Chief electrician: Heads the electrician crew. Also called the *Gaffer*.

Cinematographer: The director of photography.

Circus: The area where power trailers, change rooms, honey wagon, and portable offices are located. Also called *base camp*.

Close-up (CU): Camera term for tight shot of shoulders and face.

Cold read: Unrehearsed reading of a scene, usually at an audition.

Commission: Percentage of a performer's earnings paid to agents or managers for services rendered.

Composite: A series of photos on one sheet representing an actor's different looks.

Conflict: Status of being paid for services in a commercial for one advertiser, thereby contractually preventing performing services in a commercial for a competitor.

Copy: The script for a commercial or voiceover.

Coverage: All camera shots other than the master shot; coverage might include two-shots and close-ups.

Craft services: On-set beverage and snack table. (Different from the caterer.) In Canada, it is also the first aid attendant.

Crane shot: A camera shot raised over or above the set or the action.

Crawl: Usually the end credits in a film or television shot that "crawl" up the screen.

Credits: Opening names in a film or television show; also refers to one's performance experience listed on a resume or in a program.

Cue: Signal, often an off-stage light or hand signal, by the assistant director to indicate an actor's entrance or action.

Cut!: The verbal cue for the action of the scene to stop. **Note:** You should never jokingly say, "cut."

Cutaway: A short scene between two shots of the same person showing something other than that person.

Dailies: Screening of the footage shot the previous day, unedited.

Day player (day performer): A principal performer hired on a daily basis rather than on a longer term contract.

Daytime drama: Soap opera

Demo tape: An audio or videotape that agents use for audition purposes.

DGA: Directors Guild of America

Dialect: A distinctly regional or linguistic speech pattern or accent.

Dialogue: The scripted words exchanged by performers.

Director: The coordinator of all artistic and technical aspects of any production.

Director of photography (DP): Supervises all decisions regarding lighting, camera lenses, color and filters, camera angle set-ups, camera crew, and film processing.

Dolly: A piece of equipment that the camera sits on to allow mobility of the camera.

Dolly grip: The crewmember that moves the dolly.

Double: A performer who appears in place of another performer.

Down stage: The area located at the front of the stage that is in front of the performer.

DP: Director of photography or cinematographer.

Dress the set: Add such items to the set as curtains, furniture, and props.

Drive-on pass: In Los Angeles, a pass to drive onto and park on a studio lot.

Dupe: A duplicate copy of a film or tape. Also called a *dub*.

8x10: Commonly used size of a performer's photos, usually in black and white.

18-to-play-younger: A performer legally 18 years old who can convincingly be cast as a younger age.

Electrician: In film, crew members that place lighting instruments, focus, and gel and maneuver the lights.

Employer of record (EOR): A US term for the company responsible for employment taxes, unemployment benefits, and workers compensation coverage.

Equity: Actors' Equity Association (AEA) Union representing theatrical actors and stage managers.

Executive producer: Person responsible for funding the production.

Ext. (Exterior): A scene shot outside.

Extra: The actors that fill in the background of a scene, such as the patrons in a restaurant. Extras have no dialogue.

FICA: Federal Insurance Corporation of America (Social Security taxes)

Field rep.: Union staff member who ensures contractual compliance on sets.

First AD: First assistant director; person responsible for the running of the set. Gives instructions to crew and talent, including calling for "first team," "quiet," "rehearsal," and "take five."

First asst. camera op.: First assistant camera operator; responsible for focusing the camera lens during the shooting of a scene. Also known as the *focus puller*.

First team: The production term for the principal actors in a scene.

4-As: Associated Actors and Artists of America; umbrella organization for SAG, AFTRA, Equity, and other performers' unions.

Forced call: A call to work fewer than 12 hours after dismissal on the previous day. *See Turnaround.*

Foreground cross: Action in a scene in which an extra performer passes between the camera and the principal actors. Sometimes called a *wipe*.

FX: Special effects

Gaffer: Chief electrician

Golden time: Contractually called 16-Hour Rule Violation for Extra Performers; overtime, after the 16th hour, paid in units of one full day per hour.

Grips: Members of the film crew who are responsible for moving set pieces, lighting equipment, dolly track, and other physical movement of equipment.

Hand model: A performer whose hands are used to double for others.

Hiatus: Time during which a television series is not in production.

Holding: The designated area to which the background performers report and stay while waiting to go on set.

Honey wagon: A towed vehicle containing one or more dressing rooms, as well as crew bathrooms.

IATSE: International Alliance of Theatrical Stage Employees; the union that represents most off-camera crew members.

Industrial: Nonbroadcast film or video, usually of an educational nature.

Inserts: Shots, usually close-ups of hands or other close business, inserted into previously shot footage.

Intint. (Interior): A scene shot indoors.

"In" time: The call time or start time; also, return time from a break.

Line producer: The producer responsible for keeping the director on time and budget; generally the most visible producer on the set.

Long shot (LS): A camera shot that captures the performer's full body.

Looping: An in-studio technique used to fix dialogue already performed during principal photography by matching voice to picture.

Mark: The exact position(s) given to an actor on a set to insure that he or she is in the proper light and camera angle; generally marked on the ground with tape or chalk.

Marker!: A verbal cue that the take has been identified on camera both verbally and with the slate board.

Martini shot: The last shot of the day.

Master shot: A camera shot that includes the principal actors and relevant background activity; generally used as a reference shot to record the scene from beginning to end before shooting close-ups and over-the-shoulders.

Matching actions: The requirement that the actor match the same physical movements in a scene from take to take in order to preserve the visual continuity.

Meal penalty: A fee paid by the producer for the failure to provide meals or meal breaks as specified by the contract.

Mixer: Chief of the sound crew; responsible for the quality of the sound recording on a shoot.

MOS **(Mit Out Sound/Motion Only Shot):** Any shot without dialogue or sound recording.

MOW: Movie of the week

NATR: National Association of Talent Representatives (US)

ND **meal (Nondeductible meal):** A 15-minute meal break provided to actors by the production company to bring actors in sync with crew break time. It must be completed within two hours of performers' call time.

Night premium: A surcharge for certain work performed after 8 p.m.

Off-camera (OC or OS/**off side**): Dialogue delivered without being on screen.

Out of frame: An actor outside the camera range.

"Out" time: The time when you are released after you have changed out of wardrobe and makeup.

Over-the-shoulder: A shot over the shoulder of one actor, focusing entirely on the face and upper torso of the other actor in a scene; generally shot in pairs so both actors' expressions can later be edited together.

Overdubbing: In-studio singing or voice work; the process of laying one soundtrack over another.

Overtime (OT): Work extending beyond the contractual work day.

PA: Production assistant

Pan: A camera shot that sweeps from side to side.

Paymaster: An independent talent payment service acting as the employer of record.

Pension and health payment: An additional amount of money paid by the employer to cover employee benefits under union contract.

Per diem: Fee paid by producer on location shoots to compensate performer for expenditures for meals not provided by the producer.

Photo double: An actor cast to perform on camera in place of another. Usually used to replace leads in long shots.

Pick up: Starting a scene from a place other than the beginning.

Picture's up!: Warning that the sequence of cues to shoot a scene is about to begin.

POV shot: Point-of-view shot; camera angle from the perspective of one actor.

Postproduction: The phase of filmmaking that begins after the film has been shot. Includes scoring, sound and picture editing, titling, dubbing, and releasing.

Preproduction: The phase of filmmaking before shooting begins; includes writing, scouting locations, budgeting, casting, hiring crews, ordering equipment, and creating a shooting schedule.

Principal: A performer with lines. Under ACTRA, this is a performer with six or more lines.

Print!: A call from the director at the end of a take that this particular take is good enough to be printed.

Producer: Often called the line producer; the person responsible for the day-to-day decision-making on a production.

Production company: The company making the film or television show.

Props: Any objects used by actors in a scene.

PSA: Public service announcement

Residual: The fee paid to performers for rebroadcast of a commercial, film, or television program.

Resume: List of credits, usually attached to an 8x10 or composite.

Rewrite: Changes in the script, often using color-coded pages to indicate most current version.

Right-to-work-states: Those states that do not honor certain union provisions.

Rolling!: The verbal cue for the camera film and audio tape to start rolling.

Room tone: A sound recording (sometimes made upon completion of a scene) to record existing noise at the location. Also called *wild track*.

SAG: Screen Actors Guild

Scale: Minimum payment for services under union contracts.

Script: The written form of a screenplay, teleplay, or radio or stage play.

Script supervisor: The crew member assigned to record all changes or actions as the production proceeds. Keeps timing of shots and can be responsible for continuity.

SDI: State Disability Insurance

Second assistant director: Often two or three on a set, they handle checking in the talent, insuring proper paperwork is filed, distributing script revisions, and anything the first assistant director needs. Actors check in with the second assistant director upon arrival on the set.

Second team!: The verbal cue for the stand-ins to come to the set and be ready to stand in.

Second unit: A crew that films action sequences and other scenes that contain no dialogue.

Segue: In film or tape editing, a transition from one shot to another.

Set: The immediate location where the scene is being filmed.

Set-up: Each time the camera changes position.

SFX: Sound effects

Sides: Pages or scenes from a script, used in auditions or (if on a film set) those scenes being shot that day.

Signatory: An employer who has agreed to produce under the terms of a union contract.

Slate: A small chalkboard and clapper device, often electronic, used to mark and identify shots on film for editing; also the process of verbal identification by a performer in a taped audition (e.g., "Slate your name!").

Speed!: A verbal cue that the audiotape is up to speed for recording.

Spiking the lens: Looking directly into the lens during a scene.

Stage right: To the performer's right side, to the audience's left side. Likewise, stage left is to the performer's left, the audience's right. Stage directions are for actors, not audiences; therefore they are always given from the actor's point of view to the audience.

Standard union contract: The standard format or contract approved by the unions and offered to performers before the job.

Standards and practices: The network television censorship departments.

Stand-ins: Extra performers used as substitutes for featured players for the purpose of setting lights and rehearsing camera moves. Also known as the *second team*.

Sticks: Slate or clapboard

Studio: A building, recording room, or sound stage that accommodates film or television production.

Stunt coordinator: The person in charge of designing and supervising the performance of stunts and hazardous activities.

Stunt double: A stunt person who performs stunts for an actor.

Stunt person: A specially trained performer who performs stunts.

Submission: An agent's suggestion to a casting director for a role in a certain production.

SW: A notation on a call sheet that an actor is starting on that day and working on that day.

SWF: A notation on a call sheet that an actor is starting, working, and finishing on that day.

Sweetening: In singing/recording, the process of adding additional voices to previously recorded work.

Syndication: Selling television programs to individual stations rather than to networks.

Taft-Hartley: A federal statute that allows 30 days after first employment before being required to join a union. This applies to the US artists' unions.

Take: The clapboard indication of a shot "taken" or printed.

Take 5!: The announcement of periodic five-minute breaks.

TAMAC: Talent Agents and Managers Association of Canada

Teleprompter: The brand name of a device that enables a broadcaster to read a script while looking into the camera lens.

Theatrical: Television shows or feature film work, as opposed to commercials.

Three bells!: An audible warning for quiet because a scene is about to be filmed.

Tight shot (Go in tight): Framing of a shot with little or no space around the central figure(s) of feature(s); usually a close-up.

Tilt: The up and down movement of a camera.

Time-and-a-half: Overtime payment of one-half times the hourly rate.

Tracking shot: A shot taken while the camera is moving, either on a dolly or mounted on a moving vehicle.

Trades: Short for "trade papers," the newspapers and periodicals such as the *Hollywood Reporter* and *Variety* that specifically feature information on the entertainment industry.

Turnaround: (a) The number of hours between dismissal one day and call time the next day. (b) To shoot a scene from another direction.

Two-shot: A camera framing two persons.

Understudy: A performer hired to do a role only if the featured player is unable to perform; used primarily in live theater.

Upgrade: The promotion of an extra performer in a scene to the category of principal performer.

UPM: Unit production manager; oversees the crews and handles the scheduling and all the technical responsibilities of the production.

Up stage: (a) The area located at the back of the stage. (b) To draw attention to oneself at the expense of a fellow performer.

VO: Voiceover; an off-camera voice coming either from an actor not in the frame or from a secondary source such as a speakerphone or answering machine.

Voucher: Time slip with all pertinent information needed for getting properly paid.

W: A notation on the call sheet indicating that an actor is working that day.

Waivers: Union-approved permission for deviation from the terms of a contract.

Walkaway: A meal break in which all cast and crew are on their own to get lunch.

Wardrobe: The clothing a performer wears on camera.

Wardrobe allowance: A maintenance fee paid to on-camera talent for the use (and dry cleaning) of talent's own clothing.

Wardrobe fitting: A session held prior to production to prepare a performer's costumes.

Weather permit call: Due to weather conditions, the production company has the option to release an actor four hours after the call time (if the camera has not started to roll) with a reduced rate of pay for the day.

W/N: Will notify; a notation on a call sheet that tells the actor that he or she will probably work that day but the specific time has not yet been decided.

Wrap: The completion of a day's filming or of an entire production.

Zoom: A camera technique with a special lens to adjust the depth of a shot, accomplished without moving the camera.